How to . . .

D0412319

get the most from your
COLES NOTES

Key Point

Basic concepts in point form.

Close Up

Additional hints, notes, tips or background information.

Watch Out!

Areas where problems frequently occur.

Quick Tip

Concise ideas to help you learn what you need to know.

Remember This!

Essential material for mastery of the topic.

Your Guide to ...

Buying
& Selling
Your Home

Financing & costs

Making an offer to buy

Preparing to sell

Tips & checklists

COLES NOTES have been an indispensable aid to students on five continents since 1948.

COLES NOTES now offer titles on a wide range of general interest topics as well as traditional academic subject areas and individual literary works. All COLES NOTES are written by experts in their fields and reviewed for accuracy by independent authorities and the Coles Editorial Board.

COLES NOTES provide clear, concise explanations of their subject areas. Proper use of COLES NOTES will result in a broader understanding of the topic being studied. For academic subjects, Coles Notes are an invaluable aid for study, review and exam preparation. For literary works, COLES NOTES provide interesting interpretations and evaluations which supplement the text but are not intended as a substitute for reading the text itself. Use of the NOTES will serve not only to clarify the material being studied, but should enhance the reader's enjoyment of the topic.

© Copyright 1998 and Published by

COLES PUBLISHING. A division of Prospero Books

Toronto – Canada

Printed in Canada

Cataloguing in Publication Data

Lees, Peter, 1939 –

Your guide to … buying and selling your home

ISBN 0-7740-0585-8

1. House buying. 2. House selling. I. Title II. Series

HD1379.L43 1998   643'.12   C98-932485-0

Publisher: Nigel Berrisford

Editor: Paul Kropp Communications

Book design: Karen Petherick, Markham, Ontario

Layout: Richard Hunt

Manufactured by Webcom Limited

Cover finish: Webcom's Exclusive DURACOAT

Contents

CHAPTER ONE

Why buy a home?

THE BIG QUESTION: TO RENT OR TO BUY?

Sooner or later most people face that big decision: "Should we continue to pay rent or should we buy our own home?" For many, the decision to buy a home is the largest and most important financial decision they will make. Regardless of whether you are considering a home in the suburbs or a "downtown" home, a condominium or a traditional single-family dwelling, a starter home or a five-bedroom mansion, you are still faced with a major financial decision. Should you invest your hard-earned money in a home or should you invest your savings elsewhere and continue to pay rent?

The answer to this question, for you, should involve a careful review of key factors:

Housing needs Do you have a family or plan to start one soon? Do you intend to work from home? Do you need a larger or different style of home for pets, cars or hobbies?

Housing dreams Everyone has a dream of an ideal home. Does your personal and financial situation give you a chance to get closer to your dream?

Personal situation Are you settled in your job and relationship, or are changes likely to be coming soon? A mortgage and house ownership are long-term commitments, despite stories people tell of profitable real-estate flips and short-term gains.

Finances Do you have enough money for a down payment? Do you make enough money to qualify for a mortgage to buy the house or condo you want?

This book cannot answer all of these questions, but it will try to help you think through the important ones and give you the information you need to make solid home-ownership decisions. In the next chapter, we'll come back to some of the personal questions. In this one, let's tackle the money issues

YOUR PERSONAL CASH FLOW

A smart answer to the rent-or-buy question requires you to figure out your cash flow. Do you make enough to afford a home, or should you continue to rent? A simple calculation comes down to this:

- What will the cash demands be to buy and maintain a home?
- What will the cash demands be to continue to rent or lease?

Naturally, these cash demands have to be balanced against your current income and your projected future income. There's no sense buying a house if your job is in jeopardy, your partner is about to stop work and have a baby or you plan to go back to school in two years. It may be wise to continue renting until you have some financial stability.

Typical cash flow comparison – monthly

	Buy ($)	Rent ($)
Mortgage/rent payment	946	825
Taxes per month	100	included
Mortgage & taxes vs Rent	1046	825
Heating	150	
Electricity	100	
Maintenance	150	
Other		
Total cash out per month	1,546	825

In this example, the mortgage payment of $946 is based on a mortgage of $135,000 at 7% amortized over 25 years. The assumed monthly costs may or may not be typical for your area. It is important to know the real monthly costs where you live, for the house you intend to buy, before you make an offer on any home.

For resale houses, most current homeowners will be able to give you an estimate of monthly costs for heating and electricity (wherever possible you should ask to see the monthly bills.) Maintenance costs can range from as little as $100 per month for a home in good condition to $500 and more for an older home that requires a lot of work.

For most young people, the simple arithmetic of monthly cash flow will show that living in an apartment is cheaper than buying a home. But immediate cash flow is only one way to calculate the true cost of owning a home. While cash flow determines whether you're going to be living on hot dogs and beans for a few years or whether you'll be able to afford the occasional dinner out, the long-term financial aspects of home ownership are a bit more complex. Let's consider the cash flow required for ownership and the cash flow required to rent over a 25-year period:

Cost to rent We'll assume rental costs based on a monthly rent of $825 with an annual rent increase of 4% per year. (These numbers are for comparison purposes only and should be viewed as estimates.)

Cost to own The costs to own are based on the preceding example of $1,546 per month. Of course, these costs will fluctuate due to changes in interest rates, taxes and the monthly expenses of maintaining a home. In the case of home ownership you have a little more control over monthly costs, since you may choose to defer a maintenance cost or to do the work yourself. You have somewhat less flexibility in a condominium arrangement (see chapter 2).

	Buy ($)	Rent ($)
Year 1 Ownership costs/rent payment	18,552	9,900
Year 2 Ownership costs/rent payment	18,552	10,296
Year 3 Ownership costs/rent payment	18,552	10,707
Year 25 Ownership costs/rent payment	18,552	25,377
Total funds paid out	463,800	412,294

Obviously, the costs of home ownership look much better when viewed over the long term – and they get better still when your home is viewed as an investment, as well as a place to live.

YOUR HOUSE AS AN INVESTMENT

What happened to the $400,000 you spent on owning a home or renting an apartment? After 25 years, the mortgage on your house is paid in full and you will have gained equity in your home approximating $150,000 or more (depending on inflation). On the other hand, the renter has accrued no equity, only a large drawerful of rent receipts. To return to our example:

	Buy ($)	Rent ($)
Down payment	15,000	
Closing costs	1,500	
25-year cash requirements of owning	463,800	
25-year cash requirements of renting		412,294
Total cash required	480,300	412,294
Equity built up in the home	150,000	
Expense	330,300	412,294

Figuring in the investment value of a small house, then, the *real* cost of home ownership is $330,300 as compared to $412,294 to rent.

Of course, these are simple comparisons that do not take into consideration any growth in the value of your home, nor does it calculate the money that could have been gained by investing your down payment elsewhere. Nonetheless, for most of history, owning a house has been considered the best investment a person can make for the long term. There are a number of solid reasons for this:

Leverage One of the most interesting aspects of buying a home is the leverage you will gain in the process. Leverage is a financial term for using a small investment to gain control of a larger investment. In the example above, an investment of $15,000 gained control of a $150,000 asset. In addition, this asset can provide a roof over your head, your own fortress, a place to raise and nurture a family and a retreat from a busy world. The value of the investment was $150,000 but any appreciation will be a return on the investment of $15,000. This aspect of leverage is what makes buying a home a powerful investment.

Long-term commitment The decision to rent or buy often comes down to this: "If we do not make a commitment to buy our own home, where will we be in 25 years?" Most of the good things in life are the result of a long-term commitment. A career takes years to build. Children take 20 years to become adults. A home is no different. Although you may buy and sell many homes, your first home is the beginning of a long-term commitment to ownership. The equity you build in your first home – and in each subsequent home you buy – will be carried over to the next home you purchase.

A forced savings plan Most people have a tough time saving. You may start a regular savings plan, but no sooner do you get started when along comes an unexpected expense or that special price on a trip to Jamaica right in the middle of a long, cold Canadian winter. If you can resist these temptations and invest your savings as a renter, you will likely be wealthier in your 50s and 60s than if you buy a home.

Unfortunately, few people are disciplined enough to do this. Financial planners often view mortgage payments as a long-term, forced savings plan. Once you sign on the dotted line for that 25-year $100,000 mortgage, those monthly payments must be made regardless of whatever else comes up. Suddenly every other payment takes second priority.

This long-term commitment to a mortgage has three advantages:

- It creates a mandatory, no-choice savings plan.
- Every mortgage payment could be considered a deposit that buys you another sliver of equity in a major asset.
- You cannot withdraw from this "savings account." There is no quick way to write a cheque or withdraw money from your home mortgage.

Equity Equity is the amount of an asset that you own. If you make a $2,500 down payment on a $20,000 car, you have a $2,500 equity (ownership) in the car. The institution that loaned you the money with the car as collateral has an equity of $17,500 in the car. Over time, your equity builds up and the equity of the bank or loan company declines ... until you own the car outright.

However, there is a significant difference between the equity you build in a car through car payments and the equity you build in a home through mortgage payments. In the case of a car you are building equity in a depreciating asset. In 10 or 20 years, your shiny new car of today will be worth $50 to a junkyard.

Homes, on the other hand, have historically appreciated in value. There is of course no guarantee that homes will continue to appreciate as they have in the past but, generally speaking, a home tends to be an asset that appreciates in value or at least maintains its value.

The other significant difference between building equity in a car through car payments and building equity in a home through mortgage payments is in the time frame. Because the amount borrowed for a mortgage is large, typically well in excess of $100,000, it takes a long time to significantly increase your equity in the home. Most of your monthly payment through the first 15 years of a mortgage goes towards interest payments. It is not until you reach year

6

15 in a 25-year mortgage that you begin to pay as much towards your principal as you pay on interest.

Appreciation Appreciation is the increase in value of an investment. If you invest $10,000 and your investment increases in value to $12,500 we have seen a 25% appreciation on our investment. A home is an investment and for most people it is the largest and most significant monetary investment they will make in a lifetime. As with every investment there are two questions involved:

Risk If we place our money in this investment, will we lose our hard-earned savings?

Profit If we place our money in this investment, will we profit from it? Will we see an appreciation of our funds?

Since the 1960s, most homeowners have seen a significant appreciation in the value of their homes. Homes purchased in the 1960s for $50,000 could be sold in the early '80s for $150,000 to $200,000. There were major forces at play in the economy, such as an exploding baby boom, inflation and major economic growth cycles that fueled these increases in value. To a large degree, these forces are behind us and it would not be realistic to expect to see such significant appreciation today.

This does not mean that a well-kept home in a good location will not appreciate in value. A home purchased today may well appreciate in value, but not at the same appreciation rates we have seen since the 1960s.

Leverage and compound appreciation As we saw earlier in this chapter, leverage is using a small investment such as a $15,000 down payment to gain control of a $150,000 home. Compound appreciation occurs when an investor gets appreciation on appreciation. As you will see below, the owner of the $150,000 home saw an appreciation of 3% in the first year of ownership. The $4,500 is added to the value of the home so in the second year appreciation is based on $154,500 and not on the original $150,000 value of the home. This is compound appreciation. Over the long term it can result in a significant return on the owner's initial investment.

THREE PERCENT AVERAGE ANNUAL APPRECIATION – COMPOUNDED

Example 1: 3% Appreciation plus compound appreciation

Year	Value of home ($)	Appreciation 3% per year ($)	Compound appreciation ($)
1	150,000	4,500	
2	154,500	4,635	9,135
3	159,135	4,774	13,909
4	163,909	4,917	18,826
5	168,826	5,065	23,891

When you purchase a home you get the benefits of both **leverage** and **appreciation**. Your real investment is your down payment, not the full price of the house. In the example above, the $4,500 appreciation in the first year is really a return on the down payment of $15,000. In theory this is a 30% profit. The reality is that if you were to sell the home after the first year, the $4,500 profit would be lost in real estate commissions, mortgage penalties and moving costs. Nonetheless, there can be a real gain here over the long term.

Since real estate has historically been a good investment because of appreciation, should this be a major factor in your decision to buy?

The best answer is no. The outstanding appreciation of real estate in the '60s, '70s and early '80s was due to social and economic factors that do not exist today. Your home may appreciate and if it does, that appreciation is an added bonus. But your home might not appreciate, or it may even lose value over time, as people who bought in the early '90s found. So the primary motivation in buying and selecting a home should be to find a home that fits your current income and meets the needs of yourself or your family.

Tax advantages Real estate, at least in the form of your principal residence, is one of the few investments left in Canada that is not subject to capital gains tax.

Assume for a moment that you found your dream home. You moved in, made your 300 mortgage payments over a 25-year period, and then you decided to sell your home and move to rental housing in British Columbia. You would have built up a 100% ownership in your home, and that money would be yours free and clear.

Of course, you could have invested your money in stocks, bonds, mutual funds or gold – but all of the increase in these investments would be taxed. The current rate is 37% or higher. As a result, you'd get to keep less than two-thirds of your gain in the investment, and you might well have been paying tax on capital gains and dividends every year along the way.

This tax advantage is why there is no investment quite like buying a home. You can use a small down payment as leverage to gain control of a major, typically appreciating asset. You can live in and enjoy that asset while you pay off a mortgage, over an extended period of time, with dollars that you would have spent on rent.

ALL THE OTHER FACTORS

With this lengthy discussion of long-term finances, you mustn't forget that there are other factors in the decision on whether to rent or to buy at any given time:

* Do you have enough money for the down payment?
* Will you have cash left for emergencies if something goes wrong?
* Is the current housing market too hot, meaning you won't get good value for your money?
* Are desirable homes available, or should you wait until you find one?
* Do you have the time and energy to put into finding a suitable home and handling the problems of buying and moving in?
* Can you and your partner agree on the home you want?
* Is the stability of owning a house a good thing for you and your family – or are you better off with the flexibility of renting?

It's always wise to go into home buying with your head as well as your heart. Think through the finances carefully, review the material in this book and then make an intelligent choice.

CHAPTER TWO

Defining your ideal home

The first step in finding your next home, a home that fits your budget and lifestyle, is to define what you want and what you need in your ideal home:

- Where would you prefer to live?
- What type of home would be best for you and your family?
- Should you buy a brand-new home or would an older home be better?
- What condition would you like you new home to be in?

Finances remain a factor in making any final decision, but first you need to imagine the home that you want.

LOCATION, LOCATION, LOCATION

Location is obviously one of the most important considerations in defining your ideal home. Jobs, friends and family are all parts of the equation in selecting where you would like to live. Do you want to be close to work or is a long drive all right? If you have children, do you want them to be within walking distance of school or are you comfortable with having them bused or taking public transportation? Do want to be close to your in-laws, or is some distance a better idea?

In real estate, properties are often separated into four different location categories: urban, suburban, small town, rural. There are advantages and disadvantages to each.

Urban If you work downtown, if you like a broad range of amenities all within walking distance and if you enjoy the downtown night life and entertainment, then urban is the right choice for you. There are some disadvantages to living downtown such as the challenge of parking, smaller properties, higher housing costs, and small or non-existent backyards. But for a real city-dweller, urban is the only choice.

Suburban Living in the suburbs can range from a housing development in a distant suburb to neighborhoods that are closer to the core of the city. Newer homes in the distant suburbs tend to be larger than their city counterparts in terms of living space. In addition, they are usually built on larger lots and typically have more of the latest amenities such as two or three bathrooms, spacious en suite bathrooms, family rooms, walk-out decks and even libraries or dens. They are situated in well-designed neighborhoods with schools, shopping centers, parks, playgrounds, community centers and churches all within easy driving distance.

To some, suburban will mean an older neighborhood closer to the downtown core. These older homes may not have the size or the latest amenities of brand-new homes in the distant suburbs but they are well-established homes in neighborhoods that have their own distinct identity.

Small town Many home magazines present an idealized image of living in a small town. If you are retired, semi-retired or your occupation does not demand your physical presence at a downtown office, then small-town living is an option you may want to consider. Most older small towns do not offer the conveniences you will find in suburban communities. Instead of shopping in a large mall, you may go to three or four small neighborhood stores to pick up your supplies. You may get to pick up your mail at the town's post office, located in the back corner of the general store. Living in a small town, far from the madding crowd, sounds like an idyllic lifestyle. But before you make any commitment, be sure you know enough about the town, its facilities, its shops and its people to make the right decision.

Rural A home on the banks of a rushing brook, set in rolling meadows, may sound like the idyllic setting – and for some people it is. For others, a rural setting involves too many compromises in terms of distance from work and shopping, lack of neighbors and scarcity of sports and entertainment facilities. If rural living is right for you, be prepared to take the time to find the right home in the right setting. The home you fall in love with might have been perfect for farm life 50 years ago, but now may need expensive renovations to bring it up to your standards. It is very important to have an older home carefully examined by a qualified home inspector.

If you prefer to have a new home built to your design, be prepared for the hassles of buying the property, getting it rezoned, arranging for building permits and contracting for septic systems, wells and even access roads. As a general rule, everything will take longer and cost more that the best estimates you receive.

TYPES OF HOUSES

Once you have selected the best location for your home, the next question is: "What **type** of home would be best for us?"

There are basically five types of homes, each with advantages and disadvantages:

* detached single-family home
* semi-detached or row house
* duplex
* condominium
* townhouse

A detached single family home offers the most freedom in terms of decorating, privacy, landscaping and renovation. It tends to be the most expensive option in any location; however, a single-family home usually appreciates more quickly than the other types of homes. The primary attraction of a single-family home is its privacy and your 100% ownership of the property. You own your driveway, garage and laundry room. The drawback of a detached single-family home is that you are responsible for *all* the maintenance whether it is shovelling the driveway, cutting the grass or replacing the roof.

A **semi-detached house** shares a foundation and a center wall with the house beside it. From a builder's perspective this makes better use of a lot – two homes can be built on a plot that would have held one detached single-family home. A semi-detached home offers many of the benefits of a detached single-family home: privacy, ownership of the land, your own garage, basement and laundry room. You are responsible for all maintenance of your home with the possible exception of the driveway, which you may share with your neighbor. The danger, of course, is that your common wall may not be thick enough to shield you from a neighbor you don't like.

A **townhouse** or **row house** provides many of the benefits of a single-family home or a semi-detached home but costs less. Townhouses typically consist of four to 10 units built on one long foundation and joined by common walls. They tend to be smaller than detached or semi-detached homes, ranging from 1,200 to 1,800 square feet. They typically have small backyards and single-car garages. They do appreciate along with the real estate market; however, appreciation is based on the market value of the home and townhouses in general are less expensive than their larger detached or semi-detached counterparts. Appreciation will depend on the availability of townhouses in the general area and will be strongly influenced by the maintenance of the townhouse complex.

Townhouses are excellent starter homes for small families buying their first home and a good option for older individuals or couples who do not need a lot of space and would like to avoid the care and maintenance of a detached or semi-detached home.

In some townhouse complexes, ownership includes the home and the land it occupies. Owners are responsible for their own maintenance. In other complexes, the land is owned by all residents in the townhouse complex; it is administered by a committee made up of the owners and a monthly fee is collected from all owners to cover the maintenance costs. If major renovations are required, such as a new roof, all owners may be responsible for a portion of the cost.

Before buying a townhouse, it is important to understand exactly what you will own, what your monthly fees will be, how the complex is administered and what assessments you may be liable for.

A duplex, in most cases, is a detached two-family home that provides separate living space and privacy for two families. Each unit will have its own entrance; however, the occupants may share common areas such as the backyard. In most cases, the duplex is owned by its main occupant who rents out the other unit.

Ownership of a duplex can be attractive because the rental income may cover a large portion of the monthly mortgage payment. But if you like the idea of a duplex, be prepared to deal with the challenges that come with being a landlord. You may end up with tenants who are less than ideal or you may have difficulty collecting the rent or evicting delinquent tenants. On the other hand, you may find your tenants not only pay for more than their half of the unit, but become friends and allies in looking after the house.

Advantages of renting part of your home

Many urban homes come with a rental apartment in a renovated basement or attic. The income from this unit can usually be added to your personal income when applying for a mortgage on the house, thus allowing you to purchase a larger home than you could otherwise. As well, a portion of your house expenses can be attributed to the rental unit, allowing for real tax savings. As time goes on, you might decide to stop renting the unit and use it yourself, but it's a good way to make first-time home ownership more affordable.

A condominium is not a particular type of home as much as a legal term for collective ownership. A condominium arrangement is a legal entity set up to own land, apartment buildings, townhouses or office buildings. These units can then be rented, leased or sold, depending on the legal set up of the condominium company.

Most people see a condominium as a single unit in an apartment building. In this case, the residents own their unit outright and share ownership of the common areas with other residents.

14

The common areas may include the foyer, exercise rooms, swimming pool, laundry rooms and parking.

A condominium is managed by a committee of residents who are responsible for overseeing maintenance, repairs and renovations. The costs of maintenance – including general repairs, snow shovelling, security, exterior care and landscaping – are covered by a monthly maintenance fee from each residence. If major renovations are required, every owner may be assessed a portion of the cost. Most condominium complexes elect their corporation board annually. Owners have a vote and the freedom to express their opinion to the board, but the decisions of the board are final. If you don't like their decision, your only real choice is to move out.

Owning your own condo gives you the freedom to decorate your unit as you see fit, and your monthly payment builds your equity as opposed to building equity for a landlord. A condominium can be a good long-term investment, but it is important that the condominium complex be well maintained, and that its financing be on a firm footing.

STYLES OF HOMES: WHAT WORKS FOR YOU?

Single-family detached homes are available in three basic styles with, of course, several variations:

One-storey bungalows, as a general rule, tend to be smaller homes with smaller rooms all on one level. A bungalow can be an excellent starter home for a small family or a good retirement home when the family has grown up and moved on. There are some real advantages to having everything on one level – no stairs to climb for older people and no stairs to fall down for little ones.

Split-level homes come in several variations. The most common split-level has the main floor on its first level. When you walk in the front door, you usually go up several steps to the main level or down several steps to the basement. Most split-level homes use the basement for family rooms and utility areas. From the main level, you go up several steps to the third level with three to four bedrooms. Split-levels provide a feeling of space and freedom that you may not experience in a bungalow, which has all the rooms concentrated on one floor.

Two storey homes use the main floor for the kitchen, living room, dining room and family room. The second floor is used for three or four bedrooms. The major advantage of a two-storey home is that it provides more separation between the living and sleeping quarters than either a bungalow or a split-level home.

NEW OR RESALE?

Now that you have selected the type of home you prefer, the time has come to choose between a new home and a resale home. There are advantages to both:

Advantages of a new home With a brand-new home you can start from the very beginning and decorate it exactly as you want. You can specify types of flooring, fireplace or staircase and determine the level of finishing that you can afford. While these choices aren't endless, most builders offer a good selection. You can see some of the options when you tour the model home in a new development.

If you prefer a new home, be prepared for the ongoing construction you will find all around you as your home goes up. Chances are that your lawn will not be in when you are, your driveway will be gravel and the street will turn into a sea of mud whenever it rains or snows. If things are going to go wrong with a house, they will appear in the first one to two years after construction. As the house settles, you may find cracks appearing in the walls or in the basement. Usually these are covered under new home warranties.

New homes will have more modern conveniences and better insulation and energy efficiency. However, there are additional expenses associated with a new home that you will not usually find in an older home. You may have to spend additional money for appliances, curtains, drapes, landscaping, air conditioning, etc. On the other hand, once you move in, your new home will often be maintenance-free for 10, 15 or 20 years.

Advantages of a resale home The major advantage of a resale home is that you will be moving into an established neighborhood. Your lawn is green, your shrubs are growing, your driveway is paved and your trees are well enough established to give your street a feeling of permanence.

In terms of an investment, a resale home will often give you more for your money than a brand-new home. Many owners put thousands of dollars into home improvements ranging from small items, such as landscaping, to major projects, such as a finished basement. Although these improvements will make the home more attractive to potential buyers, they may not increase the market value of the home. A $30,000 swimming pool or a $12,000 finished basement or even $5,000 worth of shrubs and landscaping may make a home very attractive, but they will not necessarily increase the market value of a home. As a buyer, you get the home at its real market value, which is based on comparable homes for sale or recently sold in the neighborhood. All those expensive extras – which would cost you tens of thousands of dollars to order in a new home – may come with a resale home at little or no cost.

One final bonus: there's currently no GST on a resale home. That's a 7% advantage over buying a new home. (Remember that most builders include the GST in their prices.)

CONDITION: HOW MUCH WORK DO YOU WANT TO DO?

Move-in Most homes on the market are in move-in condition. The owner will have made at least cosmetic improvements so that the home will "show well" and get the highest possible price. Move-in condition means that you might want to repaint a few rooms, or hang up some new curtains or even replace the kitchen cabinets, but essentially you could move in tomorrow and be comfortable.

If both partners are working at full-time jobs, if there are several children to care for or perhaps a new baby on the way, move-in condition is by far the best option.

Fix-up A small percentage of homes on the market will not be in move-in condition. A home may be under power-of-sale and the prior owners will not see a cent from its sale – so they don't care about the home's condition. In fact, in some cases, prior owners of power-of-sale homes may have torn out major items such as sinks or bathtubs and all the light fixtures. Or a home may have been rented by an absentee owner who was not around to see the damage that the renters were doing to the home. Now the home is on the market and it needs a *lot* of work. You would not even think about moving your family into this home until you made some major changes.

 Fix-ups need imagination

When you first walk into many fix-up homes, you will feel discouraged. You may wonder, "How could anybody ever do this to a home?" But if you have the tools, skills, time and patience, you can take a fix-up home and restore it to live-in condition, purchasing it at 10–30% below what its market value would be if it were in good condition.

IMAGINING YOUR IDEAL HOME

This section provides you with an important guide in selecting your ideal home. Here are a series of checklists that will help you decide what you would like to have in the home that you buy. The features are divided into three categories:

1. **Must-have** is a feature that you and your family see as necessary. For instance, if you work out of your home, a den or office is a must-have. A must-have is a feature on which you cannot compromise.
2. **Would-like** is a feature that you would prefer. However, if everything else in the home were perfect, you could live without this feature. If you always wanted hardwood floors, but the home you are considering has good wall-to-wall carpeting, you may compromise on the hardwood floors.
3. **Nice-to-have** is an item that is not very important to you. If the home offers it – great. However, it will not be a major influence in your selection of one home over another.

Only you can make these choices. As you begin to visit homes, you can use your design guide as an evaluation tool. Does the home you are considering include all your must-haves? How many of your would-likes does the home offer? What nice-to-haves does the home offer?

Interior: Major Features	Must-have	Would-like	Nice-to-have
Number of bedrooms	☐	☐	☐
Number of bathrooms	☐	☐	☐
Main-floor bathroom	☐	☐	☐
En suite bathroom	☐	☐	☐
Eat-in kitchen	☐	☐	☐
Separate dining room	☐	☐	☐
Den or home office	☐	☐	☐
Main-floor utility room	☐	☐	☐
Central air conditioning	☐	☐	☐
One or two car garage	☐	☐	☐
Access to home from garage	☐	☐	☐
Finished basement	☐	☐	☐
Basement apartment	☐	☐	☐
Other features:			
_____	☐	☐	☐
_____	☐	☐	☐
_____	☐	☐	☐
_____	☐	☐	☐

Interior:

Secondary features	Must-have	Would-like	Nice-to-have
Large closets	☐	☐	☐
Closet near main entrance	☐	☐	☐
Large kitchen cupboards	☐	☐	☐
Appliances included:			
Stove	☐	☐	☐
Refrigerator	☐	☐	☐
Freezer	☐	☐	☐
Microwave	☐	☐	☐
Dishwasher	☐	☐	☐
Clothes washer	☐	☐	☐
Dryer	☐	☐	☐
Window air conditioners	☐	☐	☐
Double-glazed windows	☐	☐	☐
Fireplace in living room	☐	☐	☐
Fireplace in family room	☐	☐	☐
Wall-to-wall carpeting	☐	☐	☐
Drapes or blinds	☐	☐	☐
Hardwood floors	☐	☐	☐
Other features:			
_____	☐	☐	☐

Exterior:

Major features	Must-have	Would-like	Nice-to-have
Large lot (backyard)	☐	☐	☐
Fenced backyard	☐	☐	☐
Deck/patio	☐	☐	☐
Siding (brick, aluminium, wood)	☐	☐	☐
In-ground swimming pool	☐	☐	☐
Front porch	☐	☐	☐
Mature trees/landscaping	☐	☐	☐
Other features:			
_____	☐	☐	☐

Location: Major features	Must-have	Would-like	Nice-to-have
quiet street	☐	☐	☐
A mature neighborhood	☐	☐	☐
Close to:			
Work	☐	☐	☐
Schools	☐	☐	☐
Hospital	☐	☐	☐
Park/playground	☐	☐	☐
Shopping	☐	☐	☐
Major-access road	☐	☐	☐
Major highway	☐	☐	☐
Public transportation	☐	☐	☐
Other:			
_____	☐	☐	☐
_____	☐	☐	☐

Location: Secondary features	Must-have	Would-like	Nice-to-have
Close to:			
Golf course	☐	☐	☐
Tennis courts	☐	☐	☐
Skating rinks	☐	☐	☐
Swimming pool	☐	☐	☐
Library	☐	☐	☐
Community center	☐	☐	☐
Places of worship	☐	☐	☐
Theatres/restaurants	☐	☐	☐
Other:			
_____	☐	☐	☐
_____	☐	☐	☐

A few of the homes you look at will have features that, to some individuals, will be negative factors and may present problems. To others they will be no problem at all. A home directly across from a shopping mall, for instance, will be a major advantage if you work in the mall. It can be a major problem if you have small children and are concerned about the traffic.

Other factors	Problem	OK
Close to:		
a shopping mall	☐	☐
a school	☐	☐
a park	☐	☐
a main street	☐	☐
a highway	☐	☐
a community center	☐	☐
Hydro towers with heavy lines	☐	☐
Manufacturing plants	☐	☐
Public transportation route	☐	☐
Heavy truck traffic	☐	☐
Railway tracks	☐	☐
Water (river, stream, lake)	☐	☐
Other items:		
_____	☐	☐
_____	☐	☐

Is there really a home of your dreams out there? Probably, but probably not at a price you can afford. The trick is to keep looking until you can find as many features as you want at a price you can live with.

CHAPTER THREE

Shopping for your home

This is the fun part. You are going to visit many homes, see many different decors, be faced with a bewildering array of opportunities and then choose your home for the next two to three years, or seven to 10 years or even longer. If you have done your homework you will be much better prepared. You will not be wandering blindly from home to home, since you will have your checklists from the last chapter to assist you in finding your new home.

Your best guide to buying your new home will be a professional - ideally a seasoned real estate agent who will spend many hours with you in selecting your home and provide invaluable advice in making your offer. The good news is that this experienced guide comes at no cost regardless of the number of hours the agent may spend working with you. Your first task in finding a new home is to choose a real estate sales representative who likes to work with buyers and is prepared to spend whatever time it takes to assist you in finding your new home.

REAL ESTATE AGENTS – GET SOMEONE ON YOUR SIDE

The first clue as to the capabilities of any real estate agent will be how much time he or she spends with you reviewing your requirements *before* you start to drive you around looking at homes. Nothing can be as tiring and annoying as looking at homes that are of absolutely no interest to you. A good real estate sales representative will spend enough time with you to find out what you really want and will then suggest homes that fit your criteria. If the sales representative wants to get you in his car to start looking at homes before he has a solid understanding of your requirements – find another agent.

A professional real estate agent will want clients to know about an agent's legal, moral and ethical responsibilities. This is true whether the agent represents you – and splits the final commission with a selling agent – or represents the person or company selling you a house.

Of course, these roles differ somewhat. A real estate company may be an agent of the *buyer*, you. In this case, the realtor:

- represents the best interests of you, the buyer
- has a formal relationship with the buyer, for a given period of time, through a written contract that commits you to work exclusively with the realtor and commits the realtor to work on behalf of you, the buyer
- keeps you informed of any information that could influence your decisions, such as the value of comparable homes
- maintains the confidentiality of information discussed with you and is not under any obligation to share that information with the seller
- assists in determining how much you can afford to spend on a home
- will help you complete the forms for an offer to purchase the home
- is obligated to share with you any information offered by the seller. (For instance, if the seller states that they are under pressure to move by a certain date, the buyer's agent must share that information with the buyer.)

Assuming that you have chosen a good real estate agent, you'll likely want to share some of the conclusions and checklists in the last chapter. You'll definitely want to talk about the location and types of homes you have in mind, and the price you're comfortable in paying. Honest discussion ahead of time will save both you and the agent a great deal of useless home tours.

If you are shown a house at an open house, or by answering a newspaper ad or at a model home, the agent showing you the house is acting as an agent for the vendor. As a customer, you are entitled to honesty, integrity and any information about the property pertinent to your consideration. But you'd be best advised to keep quiet when touring the house. Cries of delight or phrases like "I just love this house; we *have* to buy it" will be dutifully reported back to the sellers. This may well make it difficult to get a good deal when negotiations begin.

Under the terms of a buyer's agreement:

- Your agent has a clear and direct responsibility to act in your best interest.
- Your agent is not obligated to share with the seller any information discussed with you.
- But you have an obligation to work exclusively with your agent for the term of your agreement. This doesn't cost you or the seller anything, since your agent and the vendor's agent will end up splitting the fee.

If you make an arrangement with a real estate agent to represent you, does this restrict you from buying any house that you like? The answer is no, but it does mean that your agent gets a cut of any commission in the final sale. For instance, if you drive by an open house, decide to view it and then fall in love with the house, all it takes is one phone call and your agent will work with you to place an offer on the house and to negotiate the best price and terms for you. Ultimately, the services of your agent will cost you no more – and may save you money in the bargaining phase – than if you tried to deal with negotiations yourself.

Occasionally, a real estate company will be the agent of both the vendor and the purchaser. This is called "dual agency." As a dual agent, the realtor is obligated to represent the best interests of both the buyer and the seller. If the sales representative is showing a home that has been listed by her office, she is in a dual agency relationship. The sales representative owes full disclosure of the dual agency to both the buyer and the seller. Any confidential information shared with the sales representative by the buyer or the seller must be shared with both parties. Under a dual agency relationship, it is important to understand that the sales representative has a legal obligation to share all information with both parties.

WHO PAYS FOR THE AGENT'S SERVICES?

- **The seller's agent** receives a fee or a commission from the seller of the property. This fee is clearly specified in the listing agreement.
- **The buyer's agent,** in most cases, will be paid a commission by the seller from the proceeds of the sale. Often this is a split fee with the vendor's agent.

Most real estate fees and arrangements are open to negotiation. At the present time, they range from a no-frills commission of 3% to a standard fee of 5% or 6%, depending on where you are shopping for a house.

House nicknames

As you look at homes give the each one a nickname – this will help you to remember each home you visit. Looking at several homes or more as you investigate the market can be confusing and you may find yourself unable to remember which home had which features, where it was located and why you liked it. When you give a home a nickname, such as "green door" or "big tree," you will find it much easier to picture the home and remember its features.

When you visit a house for sale, the agent will walk you through the home, talk about its features, offer you a copy of the listing and sometimes offer a computer printout of similar properties that have sold recently. If you are touring with your own agent, the sales pitch will be less obvious than if you are with the vendor's agent. Nonetheless, what you hear will be a pitch. The better your agent, the more he will be looking after your interests.

How many houses you look at, how long you hunt for a home, how carefully you examine each house – these choices are up to you. Some people, moving from out of town, have to survey all the available real estate and make a choice in a single weekend. Others, already living in a pleasant home, may take months or years to look through houses, consider neighborhoods and make various kinds of low-ball or highly conditional offers before ultimately buying a new home.

VISIT, VISIT, VISIT

One truism in the real estate industry is that serious buyers will visit a home three to five times before they put in an offer. The first visit is usually a cursory inspection – a look at the model home or a drop into an open house. The second visit is getting more serious – a careful look at closets and heating systems, the garden out back and what the neighbors seem to be like. The third visit is often the point of decision, when the buyers ask, "Could we live in this home?"

That last question is vitally important. Every home has a certain "feel." Every buyer has a certain set of preferences. The match between home and buyer requires attention to the material aspects of the deal – financing, location, what the house offers – but for long-term happiness in a home, your emotional response has to be acknowledged. It's fair to say "I'm not interested" for any number of seemingly insubstantial reasons – the house faces west and you want one that faces south; the windows are too small or too large; the people next door seem too rowdy. A smart buyer shops with the head, but the final thumbs-up must come from the heart.

Many buyers, especially first-time buyers, will want help in making the decision to put forward an offer. This is where fourth, fifth or even more visits come in. Parents, co-workers and friends can all offer advice on whether a home would be suitable for you. There's no reason why these people shouldn't come along on an inspection.

For a resale home, a professional home inspection before the deal is closed often becomes one of the conditions placed in an offer to buy. But there's no reason you can't bring along a contractor or building tradesperson to offer advice before the offer goes in. If renovations are going to be necessary, you need a ballpark figure on what they're going to cost in order to put forward an appropriate offer to buy.

 ## An easy structural inspection

While this 15-minute inspection isn't nearly as good as what will be done by a professional home inspector, it will give you some solid information to think about:

1. Make sure the house is plumb and level. Use a level or put a marble on a hardwood floor to see if it rolls. A house that has settled poorly will cause you many problems.

2. Check the basement carefully. Water stains on walls or rotting wood in the ceiling can be symptoms of major problems.

3. Check the furnace and air conditioner. If they've been well maintained on the outside, there's a good chance they're clean on the inside and the owners have been careful about other house maintenance.

4. Eyeball the roof. Use a pair of binoculars, if you have to, in order to check for missing or warn-out shingles. Roof repairs are costly.

5. Check the plumbing. Flush all the toilets; turn on all the faucets; make sure that any new copper or plastic piping goes all the way to the basement.

6. Check the electrical panel. Make sure the main electrical box has been updated to circuit breakers (not screw-in fuses) and has at least 100 amp. service.

Your real estate agent will explain the technical aspects of an offer to purchase, a process we'll examine in the next chapter. As part of your final home inspection, however, be sure to note down any item in the house that the current owners might be taking with them, but which you'd like to have for yourself. Technically, any item which is not part of the house, or bolted to a wall, is not included in the sale unless it's specified in the real estate listing. If you want the washer and dryer, make it a part of your offer. If you really want the chandelier that the current owners have excluded from the listing, make that part of your offer. If you feel that the stained glass hanging in the front window is essential for the house to keep its charm, make sure that it doesn't disappear in the moving van.

CONDOMINIUM ISSUES

If you're thinking about purchasing a condominium, the first step is to determine the size, price range, amenities and location you want. With this information your real estate agent can narrow down the listings that are suitable for you. Your agent will set up appointments for you to view condominiums in the same way you would view a detached home. After viewing the suites and eliminating those you aren't interested in purchasing, you need to work with your agent to research your potential purchases.

In making an offer, be sure you can obtain an estoppel certificate from the condominium corporation to ensure all maintenance fees and other payments are up to date by the current unit owner. Your will also want to review the declarations, bylaws, rules and budgets for the condominium and the amount of money in the reserve fund for future repair costs. The following checklist will assist you in evaluating all aspects of your potential purchase:

Buyer's Checklist: resale condominiums

☐ Has the condominium corporation levied any special assessments in the past two years?

☐ Are any special assessments expected in the near future?

☐ Walk through all common areas to see how well the building is maintained.

☐ Are hallways and common areas comfortably air conditioned?

☐ Check the shared areas for noise level and the number of children playing there.

☐ What kind of security does the underground garage have?

☐ Garage decay can be a major expense for owners in the future. Has it been checked lately?

☐ Are the residents living in the building in the same financial bracket as you? Wealthy residents might vote for changes that could be prohibitively expensive. Lower-income residents might vote down changes you would consider essential and imperative.

☐ Condominiums are a community with their own personality. Will you fit in comfortably with the other residents?

☐ Examine the corporation's budget and audited financial statements with your lawyer.

New condominiums If you would prefer to purchase a new condominium unit, you will want to review the new projects in the locations you prefer. New projects usually come with packets full of information about floor plans, amenity lists and costs. Because a new condominium project is not complete, you should go through the list provided on the following pages very carefully to make sure your choices - based on drawings and promises - will be good ones.

After you know the estimated taxes and common expenses, calculate that you have the financial ability to make the purchase and work out the details of the mortgage, then you're ready to make a deposit on your suite. The Condominium Act protects buyers of new condominiums, so you have a 10-day cooling-off period when it is possible to change your mind and have your deposit refunded. Far better, of course, to make your decision properly before putting in an offer.

Buyer's checklist: new condominium

- ☐ Survey the developer's other projects. Did they deliver their buildings on schedule?
- ☐ Ask your realtor and lawyer about additional start-up costs, such as extra fees to establish the reserve fund, disbursements, New Home Warranty Program, etc.
- ☐ Check the value of your condominium by comparing the price per square foot with other suites and projects you've seen.
- ☐ If paying cash, review your offer to purchase with your lawyer for provisions on "phantom mortgages."
- ☐ Does the builder pay interest on your deposit before occupancy?
- ☐ Ask the realtor for a profile of current buyers to determine your compatibility.
- ☐ How much of the land will be landscaped?
- ☐ Have the realtor clarify the sales brochure information.
- ☐ What will the "fully equipped" exercise room contain?
- ☐ How will common areas be furnished?
- ☐ Does the corporation have a proposed operating budget? If so, request a copy.

The site

Is the building's location close to ... ?

schools ☐   shops ☐   churches ☐   transit ☐   highways ☐

- ☐ If the project has commercial space, is access to the residential section well controlled?
- ☐ Ask if there are any proposed developments for green space and undeveloped land in the area!

Is parking included in the purchase price?   ☐

Can you buy or rent more parking?   ☐

- ☐ How many visitor parking spaces are there?

The building

☐   Is the building soundproof? How was this done?
☐   How many residents are owners compared to tenants?

What is the condominium management firm's track record?

Do they have financial expertise?   ☐

Are they experienced managers?   ☐

Do they have high maintenance standards?   ☐

What amenities and services are offered?

Do they suit your needs?   ☐

Are there any "extra fees"?   ☐

Are there any restrictions on hours?   ☐

Your security concerns are important and legitimate

Are there in-suite alarms? ☐   TV surveillance? ☐
A manned gatehouse? ☐   Controlled access? ☐

The suite

What views and sunlight will your suite have?
How close is your suite to … ?

Elevators ☐   Garbage disposal ☐   Fire exits ☐

Compare the square footage of the suite with that of your current home or apartment.

Will it be sufficient?   ☐

Will you have in-suite storage?   ☐

Is there a fee?   ☐

Are there storage facilities in the building?   ☐

Check all documents for regulations that don't suit your lifestyle. There may be restrictions in areas such as the number of people allowed per suite, pets, leasing of units, etc.

☐ How much are the maintenance fees and what does the amount cover?

☐ Are the building's utilities individually metered?

☐ What are the estimated or current property taxes?

Many insurance companies offer special condominium suite packages.

☐ Determine what the corporation's insurance will cover.

☐ What kind of policy will you need for your suite?

☐ What are the closing and scheduled occupancy dates? Are they suitable?

Review all documents with a lawyer who understands condominiums.

A handy form to remember your impressions

Address _____

House nickname _____

Listed description _____

_____

What we like/don't like about this home/condo

1. _____

2. _____

3. _____

4. _____

5. _____

6. _____

7. _____

8. _____

9. _____

Would we make an offer?   Y / N

CHAPTER FOUR

Making an offer

Any major move in life – that first day at a new school, your very first date, getting married or having your first baby – creates stress. Making all the choices and going through the search process for a new home is no exception. Buying a home can be very tough on you and your relationship. But don't panic. If this book has done its job, then you will have stepped through a well-organized process in defining and selecting your next home:

- You defined what you wanted.
- You found the best home available in the time you had.
- Now you're ready to make the offer.

Making the right offer can have important ramifications. A properly positioned offer can get you the home that you have selected on the terms that you want, and it can save you thousands of dollars.

Remember, an offer to purchase a property is a binding legal agreement. It is not something that should be entered into carelessly. Once your offer is made and accepted, it becomes a legally binding contract between you and the vendor. Both parties are expected to act in good faith to finalize the sale as agreed to in the final offer.

In the real estate business, offers come with a number of terms attached. You should think about each of these before you sign off on hundreds of thousands of dollars.

Unconditional offer You've arranged financing, think the house is great and are ready to move in, as is. This is the strongest offer a buyer can put forward.

Conditional offer You have to sell your current house or arrange financing or have a professional check out the house you want, but you're prepared to deal at the price you set. This may or may not induce the seller to agree to sell to you.

Low-ball offer You've found a house that's been on the market for quite a while and want to pick it up cheap. You're not offering much money, but maybe the seller will agree.

Counter offer Usually the seller comes back asking for more money, or changing some conditions. There can be another offer from you, another counter offer from them, all as part of an elaborate dance that can go on for a week or more.

The real question, of course, is how much you want the house and what position you're in to buy it. Money in the bank, an open time frame and a prearranged mortgage put you in a very strong position as a buyer. On the other hand, if you need a VTB mortgage (explained later on) or secondary financing, or if you have to sell your house, the vendor may decide to wait for other offers rather than agree to sell to you.

THE VOCABULARY OF AN OFFER

Your real estate sales representative will prepare your offer with you on a standard "Agreement of Purchase and Sale" from your provincial or local real estate board. All the changes, modifications, additions, deletions, offers and counter offers will be made on the original offer form. If a new form is introduced, the vendor/seller will want to review it carefully, which may result in more questions and more time being lost in the process.

Here's the vocabulary you'll find in the standard Agreement of Purchase and Sale:

Parties to the offer The offer identifies all parties involved in the offer to buy and sell.

Purchaser The purchaser or purchasers (that's you or you and your partner) must be shown on the offer.

Vendor The vendor/seller must be shown on the offer and the property must be described exactly as it is on the property deeds.

Listing broker The listing broker's name must be shown on the offer.

Co-operating broker The selling broker's name must be shown on the offer.

Price The price you are offering is shown very close to the top of the page. It is the first thing most sellers look for. In a hot market, you'll have to offer a figure very close to the asking price. In a very hot market, you might have to go over the asking price to get the house of your dreams. On the other hand, in a slow market you can often go $10,000 or more below the asking price and still reach an agreement.

Deposit You will be expected to include a deposit along with your offer. It must be large enough to demonstrate that you are serious about proceeding with the sale – usually about 5% of the purchase price.

Your deposit cheque will be made out to the listing broker who will place the deposit in trust once the deal is completed. (If there are offers and counter offers, your cheque stays uncashed until both parties reach agreement.) When the sale is closed, your deposit will be credited towards the purchase price together with interest. If your offer is not accepted or if the conditions of your offer are not met, the full deposit will be returned to you, usually without the funds ever leaving your bank account.

The house and property The offer should show, as accurately as possible, the exact legal description of the property. This entails the address, lot number, plan number, dimensions of the lot and, in some cases, a description of the property. Your lawyer will verify that the description of the property is specific and accurate.

Inclusions There will be room on the offer to add any items that you would like to see included in the sale. For instance, the washer and dryer may not be shown on the listing. However, you may want them to stay and to be included in the price you are offering. Now is the time to add any items that you would like to see included.

Fixtures   A fixture is a permanent feature of the property – anything that is attached to a ceiling or wall – and these stay with the property when it is sold. Light fixtures, bathroom accessories and wall-to-wall carpeting are considered fixtures that would normally stay with the house. However, the owner may have designated certain fixtures, such as a chandelier, as "not included" in the sale.

Chattels   Chattels (called "moveables" in Quebec) are items not considered to be a permanent part of the property. Chattels include items such as washers, dryers, stove, refrigerator, blinds, area rugs and drapes. You must be explicit in listing what chattels you would like included in the sale, right down to make, color and location. A checklist is included in this chapter for you to review in preparing your offer.

Removal of items   You may want to specify that certain items be removed as a condition of your offer, items such as an above-ground swimming pool or old wall-to-wall carpeting.

You'll have help in all this

If all these legal and strategy considerations seem complicated, don't worry. Your real estate agent will guide you through the process and will usually offer good advice on how to reach an agreement and close the deal.

CONDITIONS

There are certain standard conditions that must be included in every offer (a closing date, for instance) and there are specific conditions that you may want to add for your own protection. Here are the usual ones:

Completion date or closing date   Your offer must specify when you are prepared to close. This date may be anywhere from one to three months or longer from the date of your offer. You must allow enough time for your lawyer to complete the searches and documentation required. As a general rule, your lawyer will want 30 days to put in place all the searches, documentation and registrations that are required for the closing.

Time limit on the offer   Your offer is always irrevocable up to a specified date and time, such as 6 p.m., Wednesday, March 15, after which time it is null and void. The time you allow the vendor/seller to consider your offer will depend on the circumstances. It may be as short as a few hours or as long as 48 hours. There is no standard time period. You want this time period to be as short as possible, so that other buyers do not have time to submit offers that may be more attractive than yours.

Inspection   Many offers on resale homes are conditional on a professional inspection of the property. The inspection must be completed within a specified time period, such as three to five days after coming to terms on the sale. It's often a good idea to pick your house inspection company in advance since there won't be time to shop around after the completing your deal.

Financing   An offer is often conditional on the securing of financing at a specified term and interest rate within a given number of days. This condition covers you in case your bank refuses to do a mortgage for you to buy the house at the price you agreed on. Some financing conditions may include a vendor-take-back mortgage for a specified term and interest rate.

Assumed mortgage   If you're going to take over the vendor's mortgage, or blend it with a new one, this condition allows time for those arrangements to be made (and protects you in case there's a problem with any of this).

Sale of current home   If you need to sell your current home before completing the deal on the new one, this condition gives you time to do that. It also tends to weaken your offer (since the vendor may have to wait months before knowing if you can complete the deal), but it may be necessary to prevent you ending up with two homes at the same time.

Lawyer's review You may specify that the offer is conditional no your lawyer's review of form and content within a very short period of time, such as 48 hours. Failing this, the deposit will be returned.

Your own conditions In submitting your offer, you will want to add conditions to protect yourself. These conditions may include inspection, financing and a lawyer's review. You may have concerns, for example, about the land survey, a well on the property or the availability of natural gas. By specifying your concerns as a condition of the purchase, you guarantee that there will be no unfortunate surprises after closing.

Considerations for rural properties

Your real estate agent is the best guide for the special concerns in a particular rural area. But here are three items that may need checking before you close the deal:

- Well record – water-quality sample
- Sewage arrangements – septic system certificate of condition
- Easements on the property – who else has a legal right-of-way

CHECKLIST FOR YOUR OFFER

Before you sign and submit your offer, consider adding some of the following items that you may want to see included in the transaction. What may seem a fixture to you may seem a chattel to the current owner. A careful offer will make sure that nothing important goes off in the moving van.

	Yes	No
Above-ground swimming pool	☐	☐
Alarm system	☐	☐
Appliances:	☐	☐
Clothes dryer	☐	☐
Clothes washer	☐	☐
Dishwasher	☐	☐
Freezer	☐	☐
Refrigerator	☐	☐
Stove	☐	☐
Range and built-in oven	☐	☐
Barbecue	☐	☐
Ceiling fans	☐	☐
Central vacuum attachments	☐	☐
Electric light fixtures	☐	☐
Custom-built shelving	☐	☐
Draperies, blinds, curtains	☐	☐
Electronic air cleaner	☐	☐
Broadloom	☐	☐
Garage door opener	☐	☐
Gardening tools, lawnmower	☐	☐
Playground equipment	☐	☐
Satellite dish and equipment	☐	☐
Snow blower	☐	☐
Space-saver drawers and shelving	☐	☐
Storage shed	☐	☐
Swimming-pool equipment	☐	☐
Water softeners	☐	☐
Window air conditioners	☐	☐

THE PROCESS OF AN OFFER

As soon as your offer is prepared and signed, your agent will contact the listing agent to arrange to present your offer to the current owner. Within the irrevocable time period you have specified, the vendor can accept the offer as is, reject it, or modify it and sign it back to you. This becomes the vendor's own irrevocable counter offer for the period of time specified.

If your offer is **accepted** right away, it should be given to your lawyer as soon as possible so that the lawyer can initiate whatever action is required. You can instruct your real estate sales representative to send a copy.

If your offer is **rejected**, you may want to resubmit it at a higher price or with a different closing date. Your real estate sales representative should have a good idea as to why the vendor rejected it and how you could resubmit the offer to get negotiations started.

If your offer is **modified** and signed back to you, as is usually the case, it indicates that the vendor is interested in proceeding with negotiations. The current owner may have signed it back at a higher price, a different closing date, with chattels removed or added or any combination of these and other items. You will have a time and date by which you must respond before the vendor's counter offer becomes null and void. You can then accept the counter offer as is. In this case, the transaction is done and you have a binding legal contract. Or you can reject the counter offer and walk away from the transaction. Usually, you'll end up modifying the counter offer and then resubmit it with a specified irrevocable time and date for its acceptance.

The process of offer and counter offer can go on any number of times until both parties agree or one party walks away from the transaction.

STRATEGIES TO GET A GOOD DEAL

In the process of buying a home, you have only one opportunity to negotiate and that is through the offer process. A good real estate sales representative will know how to strategize your offer and its presentation so that the offer process works to your advantage.

Your real estate agent should know the history of the home and should be able to answer the following questions: Has it been on the market for a long time with no activity? Is the vendor in a hurry to sell or can the vendor afford to take their time and wait for the perfect offer? Is the home overpriced or underpriced as compared with other homes in the neighborhood?

The first step in any strategy is to find out as much as you can as to why the vendor is selling. Have they purchased another home with its closing due shortly? Are they anxious to move to another city or province? If so, your first offer may be as much as 10% below the asking price. If the vendor counter-offers with a higher price, you will know that they are prepared to negotiate. If the vendor rejects the offer, you can always resubmit it at a higher price.

If your real estate agent believes that the home is priced at less than its true market value, it would be wise to offer the asking price. But you could request the inclusion of additional items such as appliances not included in the listing.

If you have prearranged financing, you might want to offer an "all cash deal" below the asking price. An all cash deal sounds a lot more attractive than an offer that is contingent on financing or dependent on a purchaser selling their current home.

Finally, you can ask that certain items be excluded from the deal and removed from the property. For instance, if there is an above-ground swimming pool, you could ask that it be removed and the price be reduced by $5,000. Given the cost of removing the pool and reassembling it elsewhere, the vendor may come back with a counter offer of $2,000 off the price with the pool left standing.

Negotiations of any kind are difficult. In a house purchase, with hundreds of thousands of dollars on the table, the tension can be grueling. Be prepared for some difficult days in order to get the house of your dreams at a fair price.

CHAPTER FIVE

Financing your purchase

The financial issues involved in buying a home really come down to two pots of dollars: the down payment and the mortgage. Both of these, of course, are dependent on the money that you make, the money you've saved and the credit history you've built up over time. But there are many choices to make, options to consider and hurdles to jump before you can afford to get the keys to your dream home.

DOWN PAYMENT

For young people buying their first home, the down payment always seems to be the first hurdle that must be cleared. For subsequent homes, you'll have the equity built up in your starter home thanks to mortgage payments and the way homes tend to gain in value over time. But for your first home, the down payment always looks like an enormous pot of money.

The standard down payment for a home with a single conventional mortgage is 25% of the purchase price. Bankers use this as a quick rule for determining how much house you can afford. If you are applying for a conventional mortgage with a 25% down payment, the price range to consider should be four times the down payment. If a couple has a down payment of $40,000, for instance, they should be looking at homes in the $160,000 range.

Some lenders provide loans to 90% of the purchase price through high-ratio or NHA mortgages (explained later on). These ordinarily cost more than conventional mortgages, but they remain an option if you want a $150,000 home and have only $15,000 in your savings account.

Often you can arrange for a second mortgage to bridge the gap between a 75% first mortgage and the 10% down payment most vendors expect. Again, this costs more than a single, conventional mortgage.

And some lenders will even offer a special mortgage, especially on a new home, that will cover 95% of the purchase price. Often these high-ratio mortgages are paid for by an inflated selling price for the house or by very high interest rates. Any deal that asks for only $7,500 and gives you the keys to a $150,000 piece of real estate should be looked at very carefully indeed.

Obviously all these scenarios require some money to be put down on the house of your dreams. The major task for first-time buyers is often in finding any money at all.

Sources for a down payment

Couples who are starting out in home ownership are often already burdened with debts. There are credit cards, student loans, car loans and timed payments for furniture and other goods. Many young couples, evaluating their net worth, would find they come up with a negative number. This makes house buying difficult, but not impossible, if you have other sources of cash or a good current income.

Here are sources for down-payment cash, from best to worst.

- **Your savings** Without a doubt, there is no stronger way to go into a house purchase than to have 25% of the money you need – anywhere from $25,000 to $100,000 or more – sitting in a savings account. At times, the government permits you to save this money and save on your taxes through an RHOP (Registered Home Ownership Program) investment. Like an RRSP, this permits you to put money aside to buy a home in the future and then deduct those savings from your taxable earnings. It's a great deal, when available.

  While these dollars may seem enormous, a young working couple can often save between $500 and $1000 a month by having money sent directly from paycheques or bank accounts into a special savings fund. In two or three years, with interest or the value appreciation in a mutual fund, this will often be enough to make a down payment on a starter home.

- **Your savings and your goods** Some young couples have other assets that can be cashed in to use towards the down payment – stocks or bonds given to you as a kid, an expensive car that can be replaced with a cheaper one, photographic or electronic gear that you may not really need or value all that much. There may be wedding gifts of considerable value that you've never used. Don't sell your grandmother's antique silver for a bargain-basement price, but do look around at what you have and may not need any more.

- **Employer assistance** Some companies will provide down-payment assistance or a mortgage interest-rate break if you are asked to move with the business.

- **Parents** At one time, many parents tried hard to provide their children with the down payment for a first house. Of course, those were the days of $30,000 houses, $1,500 down payments and 3% mortgages. Given the expense of current real estate, the gift of a full down payment is a considerable stretch for most parents. Nonetheless, many young couples get some help from their parents towards their first down payment. Only you can consider if this is a reasonable request given your family situation. But remember, when you ask your parents for cash, you're asking them to stick their noses into your life and finances. This isn't always pleasant. You'd better be prepared to show you've done some saving and a lot of planning before you make the request.

- **Other relatives** If there is an uncle or aunt in your family who is especially fond of you, these relatives might be willing to help with the down payment. (Even if they won't provide money for a down payment, such relatives might be willing to do a first or second mortgage for you – a mortgage that keeps the interest money you pay inside the family.)

- **Borrowing** You can cut the amount of the required down payment by borrowing 90–95% of the value of a house. This costs you more by the month, but might make it possible to get the house of your dreams. Just remember that you are responsible for costs on top of any down payment you need to buy the house.

You can also borrow from money saved in your RRSP, and then pay it back over a fixed period of time. In this way, you're really borrowing from yourself.

Credit cards

Despite what you see in some TV commercials, it is never a good idea to borrow a home down payment on credit cards. The interest rates are always 15% or higher. The amount you can get on one card is limited. Payment terms are terrible. Credit card borrowing is a risky way of financing a rental property; it's simply stupid for buying a home to live in.

MORTGAGES

Unless you were born rich, recently won a million-dollar lottery or have a very generous and very rich uncle, you will be faced with using a mortgage to buy your next home. The type and the size of your mortgage is a major consideration in buying a home.

You don't want to make a mistake in estimating either your needs or your finances. If you buy a home that is too small, with too many compromises, you may find yourself looking for a new home a lot sooner than you anticipated. This of course is an expensive proposition. If you take on a mortgage that is larger than you can handle, you may find yourself having trouble making the mortgage payments. This can be particularly dangerous if you are suddenly faced with an emergency that demands an immediate cash payout.

The good news is that there are proven methods to determine how large a mortgage you should assume. It is well worth your time to understand these methods so that you are comfortable with them before walking into your bank or trust company. Your mortgage institution will most certainly use these methods in determining how large a mortgage they will underwrite for you.

GROSS DEBT SERVICE RATIO (GDSR)

The first thing every mortgage lender will look at is your GDSR: the ratio of your total debt servicing requirements against your total monthly income. In general, your GDSR should not exceed 32% of your gross monthly income.

In the following example, couple A has a gross monthly income of $5,000. Their monthly mortgage and tax payments should not exceed $1,600 (32% of $5,000). Let's assume that their monthly real estate taxes will be $150. To stay within the recommended guideline of 32%, their monthly mortgage payment should not exceed $1,450. Their mortgage lender will explain that this qualifies them for a $200,000 mortgage, assuming a 7% 25-year mortgage.

Couple A	Gross Debt Service Service Ratio (GDSR)
Gross monthly income	$5,000
32% of gross monthly income	$1,600
Assuming monthly real estate taxes	$150
Income available for mortgage payments	$1,450
Qualifies for a mortgage of:	$200,000

We have used many examples throughout this book for illustrative purposes. All the figures used should be viewed as approximations.

You should review all such numbers, including your own calculations, with a real estate sales representative or mortgage specialist.

TOTAL DEBT SERVICE RATIO (TDSR)

The next measurement a mortgage lender will use is a Total Debt Service Ratio (TDSR). Your TDSR should not exceed 40% of your gross monthly family income. The TDSR takes into consideration the percentage of income committed to fixed monthly expenses including such items as car payments, credit card payments, retail account payments and any other monthly loan payments.

In the following example couple A has a gross monthly income of $5,000. They have monthly commitments as listed that total $350. Standard TDSR calculations indicate that their monthly mortgage and tax payments should not exceed $1,650 plus their current monthly commitments of $350. Their mortgage lender will explain that this qualifies them for a $215,000 mortgage, assuming a 7%, 25-year mortgage.

Couple A	Total Debt Service Service Ratio (TDSR)
Gross monthly income	$5,000
40% of gross monthly income	$2,000
Car payment	$225
Retail loan repayment	$125
Income available for mortgage and taxes	$1,650
Assuming monthly real estate taxes	$150
Income available for mortgage payments	$1,500
Qualifies for a (7%) mortgage of	$215,000

If this couple had higher monthly commitments – say they had bought an expensive new car – this would have reduced the size of mortgage they were qualified to carry.

OTHER QUALIFICATION METHODS

Your bank or other mortgage institution may use other quick methods to estimate the size of mortgage for which you qualify.

 Two and a half times your annual gross family income By multiplying your gross annual income by 2.5, you will arrive at a quick estimate of the size of mortgage you can carry. Couple A's annual gross income is $60,000. At 2.5 times their annual income, they could consider a mortgage in the $150,000 range, but it might be a financial stretch for them.

Two times your annual gross family income By multiplying your gross annual income by 2, you will arrive at a more conservative estimate of the size of mortgage you can carry. At 2 times Couple A's annual gross income of $60,000, they should consider a mortgage in the $120,000 range.

Most mortgage lenders will use the more conservative methods of determining the size of mortgage that would be appropriate. Especially for first-time owners, lenders tend to err on the side of caution. As a result, it is wise to be conservative yourself in determining how large a mortgage you can handle and how large a house you will be able to purchase.

What can you really afford?

These charts are intended to give you a very quick rough estimate as to how large a home you may be able to purchase based on your gross monthly income.

Column 1 – your current monthly gross income
Column 2 – the 30% of your gross income that would be available for
          mortgage and taxes
Column 3 – the estimated real estate taxes on your new home
Column 4 – the total available after an allowance for taxes
Column 5 – the total mortgage you could handle
Column 6 – the most expensive home you could buy with a 25% down payment
Column 7 – the most expensive home you could buy with a 10% down payment

Please remember that this is a rough estimate. Your real estate agent, mortgage broker or banker will assist you in evaluating the size home you should consider.

25-year amortization at 5% rate

Monthly Income $	30%	Taxes	$ Available	Mortgage	House price	House price
					25% down	10% down
2,000	600	200	400	68,729	91,638	76,365
2,500	750	210	540	92,784	123,711	103,093
3,000	900	220	680	116,838	155,785	129,821
3,500	1,050	230	820	140,893	187,858	156,548
4,000	1,200	240	960	164,948	219,931	183,276
4,500	1,350	250	1,100	189,003	252,005	210,004
5,000	1,500	260	1,240	213,058	284,078	236,732
5,500	1,650	270	1,380	237,113	316,151	263,459
6,000	1,800	280	1,520	261,168	348,225	290,187

25-year amortization at 6% rate

Monthly Income $	30%	Taxes	$ Available	Mortgage	House price	House price
					25% down	10% down
2,000	600	200	400	62,500	83,333	69,444
2,500	750	210	540	84,375	112,500	93,750
3,000	900	220	680	106,250	141,667	118,056
3,500	1,050	230	820	128,125	170,833	142,361
4,000	1,200	240	960	150,000	200,000	166,667
4,500	1,350	250	1,100	171,875	229,167	190,972
5,000	1,500	260	1,240	193,750	258,333	215,278
5,500	1,650	270	1,380	215,625	287,500	239,583
6,000	1,800	280	1,520	237,500	316,667	263,889

25-year amortization at 7% rate

Monthly Income $	30%	Taxes	$ Available	Mortgage	House price	House price
					25% down	10% down
2,000	600	200	400	57,143	76,190	63,492
2,500	750	210	540	77,143	102,857	85,714
3,000	900	220	680	97,143	129,524	107,937
3,500	1,050	230	820	117,143	156,190	130,159
4,000	1,200	240	960	137,143	182,857	152,381
4,500	1,350	250	1,100	157,143	209,524	174,603
5,000	1,500	260	1,240	177,143	236,190	196,825
5,500	1,650	270	1,380	197,143	262,857	219,048
6,000	1,800	280	1,520	217,143	289,524	241,270

YOUR CREDIT RECORD

Your credit record can be the most important criteria that a mortgage lender will look at in evaluating your application. Your credit history contains a detailed record of every charge account, credit purchase or credit card purchase made within the last seven years (and in some cases it will extend even further back). This credit record will show for every account:

your highest balance – our current balance – your payment record

If you ran into a cash flow problem and were late making a payment, this stays on your record. If you had a disagreement with a merchant over some goods you purchased and returned and refused to make any payments on that account, it may still be on your account as payments due and unpaid. Your account could have been charged in error, corrected by the merchant on their records but not updated to your credit record and it will be on your account as an unpaid debt at the Central Credit Bureau. If you applied for credit and were turned down, even that rejection stays on your credit record. In fact, every inquiry made against your credit file at the Central Credit Bureau remains in plain view on a computer screen.

- An R2 beside an account indicates that you were late in making payments to that account.
- An R9 beside an account indicates that you did not pay the amount due within 30 days of its due date. An R9 says to any credit officer, "This person does not pay his or her bills, and is a poor credit risk." With one R9 on your file, a lender may want to know what the story is behind it. With several R9s on your file, the lender will probably suggest that you look elsewhere for a mortgage.

If you have been turned down for credit recently, or if you have any concerns about your credit history, take the time to find out exactly what your credit file says about you. You can avoid embarrassment in applying for a mortgage by checking your credit rating first:

- Contact your local credit bureau.

- Ask to see a copy of your credit file and ask the clerk for an explanation of any accounts with an R2 to R9 beside them.
- If there is a problem, contact the merchant involved by registered mail.
- Arrange to settle the account or to clear up any misunderstandings.
- Get a statement in writing from the merchant stating that the account has been settled to their satisfaction. The credit bureau is obligated, under law, to allow you to place any statement you wish in your credit file.
- Send a registered letter along with a copy of the merchant's letter to the credit bureau and ask them to update your file to indicate that the account has been cleared up.
- Ask for written verification from the credit bureau that your record has been corrected.

UNDERSTANDING MORTGAGES

What is a mortgage? A mortgage is an investment made by an individual, a corporation such as a bank or lending institution, in you – using a house as collateral. Investors, particularly conservative investors, love the security, guaranteed return, regular payments and terms and conditions of a typical residential mortgage.

Here is a review of the terminology used by mortgage professionals. This section will not make you into a mortgage expert, but it will give you a much better understanding of the options open to you when you apply for one. To begin, imagine a line of people at a ticket counter:

First mortgage The first person in line is the holder of the first mortgage. In the event of a default (a person failing to make a mortgage payment for three months or more will trigger most mortgage holders to foreclose and take over ownership of the property), the first mortgage holder is first in line to collect his share of the proceeds from the sale of the property.

Second mortgage The second person in line is the holder of the second mortgage. In the event of default, the second mortgage holder is next to collect a share of the proceeds – but only after the first mortgage holder has been paid in full. Because of the risk, a second mortgage is usually a short-term mortgage at a higher interest rate than a conventional mortgage.

Third mortgage The third person in line is the holder of the third mortgage. In the event of default, the third mortgage holder is last to collect the share of the proceeds after the first and second mortgage holders have been paid in full. Often, there's no cash value left in the house at this point. Because of the risk, a third mortgage is usually a short-term mortgage at a considerably higher interest rate than either a conventional mortgage or second mortgage. In many cases the third mortgage holder will insist on additional collateral – your car or other investments – to secure the mortgage.

Principal The mortgage principal is the total amount of the mortgage at a particular point in time. A $150,000 mortgage would have a principal of $150,000. As mortgage payments are made, this principal amount will be reduced.

Here is a forecast of what a $150,000 mortgage (at 8.5% interest, compounded semi-annually, with a 25-year amortization) will look like over time:

At the end of Year 5 (60 payments), the principal balance will be $139,000.

At the end of Year 10 (120 payments), the principal balance will be $122,000.

At the end of Year 15 (180 payments), the principal balance will be $97,000.

At the end of Year 20 (240 payments), the principal balance will be $59,000.

At the end of Year 25 (300 payments), the principal balance will be $0.

Interest rate Interest is the lender's return on the investment and every lender will try to get the highest return possible. From your perspective, the interest rate of your mortgage can be a determining factor in buying a home. A high interest rate such as 12% will increase your monthly payment by as much as 60% over a low interest rate such as 6%. The good news is that because mortgages are such a good investment, there is always a lot of competition and interest rates for mortgages are traditionally much lower than for other kinds of debt.

Remember, the current interest rate must be factored into your GDSR and TDSR and it will play a key role in calculating how large a mortgage you qualify for.

Here is a comparison of the difference that your interest rate will make to your monthly payment. These examples assume a $150,000 mortgage with payments amortized over 25 years, with interest compounded semi-annually.

At 6% interest rate your monthly payment would be $970.

At 7% interest rate your monthly payment would be $1,070.

At 8% interest rate your monthly payment would be $1,150.

At 10% interest rate your monthly payment would be $1,350.

At 12% interest rate your monthly payment would be $1,550.

Payments Mortgage payments always include a portion paid against the principal and a portion paid out as payment. As you will already have noted, the initial portion paid against the principal is very small and the interest portion is very large. Over time, the principal payments grow larger and interest takes a small piece to the monthly mortgage payment. Mortgage payments are frequently referred to as blended payments because they are a blend of interest and principal payments.

Year	Monthly payment ($)	Payment applied to interest ($)	Payment applied to principal ($)
1	1,200	1,050	150
5	1,200	990	210
10	1,200	870	330
15	1,200	700	500
20	1,200	420	780
25	1,200	10.00	1,190

You can change the frequency of payments to weekly, rather than monthly, and thereby pay down your mortgage more quickly. Or you can shorten the amortization period by raising your payments – but cutting back on the number of years you will be paying off your house. Just don't get so ambitious paying off your house that you no longer have cash left to live a life.

Mortgage term Of all the terminology used in the world of mortgages, the "mortgage term" is one of the most confusing. The term of the mortgage is the length of time the lender is prepared to loan the money at a particular interest rate. Mortgage terms range from six months to 10 years. At the end of the term, the principal still owing must be paid back to the lender unless the lender is prepared to renew the mortgage for another term.

Which is better: a short-term mortgage or a long-term mortgage? The answer, as in so much else, depends on your situation.

A **long-term mortgage** guarantees the interest rate for the entire length of the term. For instance, a five-year term mortgage with a 6% interest rate locks the interest and the amount of your monthly payment in for five years. You have the comfort and security of knowing that your monthly mortgage payment will not change for five full years.

A **short-term mortgage** historically will have much lower interest rates and give you the flexibility to move your mortgage to another institution if you can negotiate better terms. A lower interest rate can significantly reduce your monthly payments at the start, but there's no guarantee you'll be able to make the higher payments necessary in the future if interest rates go up.

Amortization The amortization is the number of years it would take to pay off a mortgage entirely. For instance a mortgage with a 25-year amortization will take 25 years to pay off. However, a mortgage may go through many "terms" in its lifetime. These terms will make no difference to the amortization of the mortgage.

A long-amortization mortgage, such as 25 or 30 years, will have a lower monthly payment. You will be paying the principal off at a much slower rate than a mortgage with shorter amortization period.

A short-amortization mortgage, such as 15 or 20 years, will have a much higher monthly payment but the total interest paid over the full amortization of the mortgage will be considerably lower. In the example below, the difference in the total interest paid between a 20-year amortization and a 30-year amortization is $100,000.

COMPARING AMORTIZATION PERIODS
(With a $150,000 mortgage at 8.5% compounded semi-annually)

Amortization period	Monthly payment ($)	Total paid ($)	Total interest ($)
15 years	1,470	265,000	115,000
20 years	1,290	310,000	160,000
25 years	1,200	360,000	210,000
30 years	1,140	410,000	260,000

TYPES OF MORTGAGES

Conventional This is the most common mortgage used. It is based on a 25% down payment and a mortgage principal equal to 75% of the market value of the home.

High-Ratio A high ratio mortgage will be for 90-95% of the market value of the home with a 5–10% down payment. A high-ratio mortgage may carry a higher interest rate than a conventional mortgage and the lender may ask for mortgage insurance to protect against default. This insurance protects the lender, not you, the borrowers.

In the example shown below, the home has been appraised at $180,000. The buyer has $18,000 available for a down payment. As you will note, the insurance cost is $4,050 and it has been added to the mortgage principal.

Appraised value of home	$180,000
Buyers down payment (10%)	$18,000
High-ratio mortgage (90%)	$162,000
Default insurance (2½%)	$4,050
Total mortgage	$166,050

NHA (National Housing Act) mortgage NHA mortgages are high-ratio mortgages insured by the Canada Housing and Mortgage Corporation. They are designed to assist someone who does not have the 25% down payment required for a conventional mortgage. The good news is that they can help you buy your first home if you do not have a 25% down payment. The bad news is that they can be considerably more expensive due to application fees and the insurance required. (All application fees and insurance premiums are charged to you, the buyer.) The terms and conditions of a NHA mortgage may change and this option should be discussed with several mortgage professionals before you make any commitment.

VTB (Vendor Take Back) mortgage A VTB mortgage is offered by a vendor often as an inducement to sell the property. A VTB is usually a short-term mortgage of one to five years and may range from 75% of the sales price of the property to a small second mortgage of a few thousand dollars. A VTB as a second mortgage can be used to make up a portion of the 25% down payment required for a conventional mortgage.

A short-term VTB mortgage means that you will have to find another lender at the expiration of the VTB mortgage term. This can be a problem if the property is overpriced or if you're are not qualified for a mortgage large enough to cover a conventional mortgage plus replacement of the VTB mortgage.

Builder's mortgage This is similar to a VTB mortgage. A builder may offer attractive mortgages, with interest rates below current market rates, as an inducement to buy one of their new homes. These are usually short-term mortgages of one to two years.

Three things to be aware of in considering a builders mortgage:

1. If the interest rate is below current market interest rates, the builder will often have added the interest cost to the sale price of the home.
2. You may be able to negotiate a lower price on the home if you can make your own mortgage arrangements.
3. You will have to find another mortgage at the end of the term of the builder's mortgage. This could be a problem if the market price of the home two years down the line is not high enough to qualify for a mortgage to replace the builder's mortgage.

In the example below, a builder added the $8,000 interest cost to the price of the home. The home was sold for $208,000 as opposed to $200,000 with a buyer-arranged mortgage. Let's assume, when the builders mortgage term expires, that the market value of the home is not high enough to qualify for a mortgage large enough to pay off the builder's mortgage. Then you, the buyer, may be forced to take on a second mortgage at a higher interest rate *in addition* to a conventional mortgage.

Two-year term, mortgage principal		$200,000
Interest at going rate (9%)	$36,000	
Interest of builder's mortgage (7%)	$28,000	
Difference	$8,000	$8,000

Rather than take the builder's mortgage, smart buyers ask the builder to pay down the interest rate with a lender of your choice. There is no additional cost to the builder and you may be able to arrange a longer term with a lender of your choice who will, in all likelihood, renew the mortgage at the end of its term.

Fixed-rate mortgages This is a mortgage with the interest rate set for the full term of the mortgage. For example, a five-year fixed rate mortgage at 7% means that interest rate on the mortgage will not change for the full five-year term of the mortgage.

There are two advantages in a fixed-rate mortgage:

- First, your monthly payment will not change throughout the entire term of the mortgage.
- Second, even if interest rates go up, a fixed-rate mortgage will not be affected.

The interest rate will stay at the agreed percentage. If the long-term outlook is that interest rates may rise, then a fixed-rate mortgage is the best option.

Variable-rate mortgages The interest rate of a variable-rate mortgage will rise and fall based on the prime rate set by the Bank of Canada. Your monthly mortgage payment may remain the same (depending on the terms set by your lender), but if the interest rate goes up, more of your monthly payment will be allocated to interest and less to reducing the principal. If the interest rate goes down, a larger percentage of the monthly payment will be allocated to principal and less to interest.

Open mortgage A fully open mortgage can be paid off in full at any time. There are several advantages to an open mortgage:

- If interest rates drop below your current rate, you can arrange a new mortgage at a lower rate and pay off the current mortgage with no penalty costs.
- If you sell your home and move to another, you can pay off the existing mortgage with no prepayment penalties.
- If you have extra cash, you can make additional payments against the principal at any time. Prepayments go directly against the principal (not the interest) and can significantly reduce interests costs, particularly if they are made in the early years of a mortgage's amortization.

Partially open mortgage This mortgage permits prepayments against the principal within certain time frames. For instance, a partially open mortgage may allow a prepayment of up to 10% every year. In some cases, a partially open mortgage may be paid in full with no penalties or minimal penalties.

Closed mortgage A closed mortgage does not permit any pre-payments and a substantial penalty must be paid if the mortgage is paid off before the end of its term. This can be a considerable disadvantage if you are required to sell your home before the term of the mortgage is completed.

REDUCING MORTGAGE INTEREST

The total interest cost with a 20-, 25- or 30-year mortgage will be much, much higher than the original amount borrowed. Your full cost of ownership can be double or more the purchase price of a home when interest costs are taken into consideration. So how can you reduce the interests costs associated with a mortgage? Here are five ways:

1. Arrange a mortgage with a shorter **amortization**. The shorter the amortization of a mortgage, the higher the monthly payments and the lower the total interest costs.
2. Make a large **additional payment** early in the life of the mortgage. A $5,000 prepayment made in Year 2 of a mortgage with a 25-year amortization will reduce the amortization by 26 months and reduce the total interest cost by $26,000.
3. Make small **additional payments** every year through the first five years, or longer. Prepayments of $600 every year through the first five years of a mortgage with a 25-year amortization will save $16,000 in interest costs and retire your mortgage 16 months ahead of schedule.
4. Make mortgage payments every **week** instead of once a **month**. Instead of making 12 monthly payments, make 52 weekly payments. This will save a small amount in total interest costs over the amortization of the mortgage.
5. For many people a large prepayment, such as $5,000 or $10,000 can be difficult, particularly in the early years of home ownership. Even annual additional or prepayments of $2,000 through the first five years of a mortgage can be a stretch. Nonetheless, one of the best and least painful options is to combine weekly payments with accelerated payments. Take your monthly payment and divide it by four to calculate the

weekly payment and then add $50 or more, or less, to the weekly payments. The combination of high-frequency weekly payments *plus* accelerated payments will have a significant impact on the total interest cost of a mortgage. As you will see in the following example, the combination of weekly payments plus an accelerator of $50 per payment reduces the total interest cost by $25,000.

Payment frequency + accelerated payments

The combination of weekly payments plus accelerated payments will produce dramatic results with very little pain. By adding a small amount to the weekly payment, interest costs can be significantly reduced.

The following example compares a monthly payment with a weekly accelerated payment. We added $50 to our weekly payment to round it up to $330 per week, $1,320 per month. By adding $50 to the weekly payment, we reduced our total interest cost by $25,000.

Payment frequency	Mortgage payment ($)	Interest paid ($)	Payments made
Monthly	1,200	210,000	300 payments
Weekly	330	185,000	1,014 payments

Portable mortgage A portable mortgage can be moved from one home to another. This can be particularly valuable if the mortgage is below current interest rate. Other advantages are that the holder of a portable mortgage does not incur prepayment penalties in paying a mortgage off before its term expires. Nor do you face the costs of arranging a new mortgage when you sell one home and move to another.

Blended mortgage A blended mortgage is the result of combining an existing mortgage with a new mortgage. In the example below, the current owners of a house have a $100,000 mortgage at 6%. The buyers arrange for their lender to combine the existing mortgage with a new $50,000 7.5% mortgage. The result is a blended mortgage of 6.5%. (**Note:** This is possible only if the $100,000 mortgage is portable.)

Current mortgage	$100,000 at 6%
New mortgage	$50,000 at 7.5%
Blended mortgage	$150,000 at 6.5%

The buyers' blended mortgage is 1% below current mortgage rates. This percentage results in a monthly interest savings of approximately $90.

Assumable mortgage This mortgage stays with the home and a buyer can take it over or "assume" it. The buyer may still have to meet the mortgage holder's qualifications, but usually this is not a problem. An assumable mortgage can be an attractive selling feature of a home if it is a long-term low-interest mortgage. In the example below, a couple is buying a $150,000 home with an assumable five-year mortgage of $80,000 at 5.5%. They have $40,000 available as a down payment.

How can this couple use this assumable mortgage to their advantage? If current interest rates are running around 7%, they may be able to arrange a second mortgage of $30,000 to make up the difference between their $40,000 down payment plus the $80,000 assumable mortgage and the $150,000 selling price.

Current $80,000 mortgage	5.5%
Second mortgage of $40,000	7.0%
Their effective blended mortgage interest rate	6.0%

Instead of a $120,000 mortgage at the current mortgage interest rate of 7%, the buyers were able to arrange an effective mortgage rate of 6%.

Prearranged mortgage   Most mortgage institutions offer a pre-arranged mortgage. A prearranged mortgage means that the mortgage institution has reviewed the prospective buyers' financial position and credit standing and approved you for a mortgage up to a certain amount.

A prearranged mortgage can be an important tool for you in making an offer and negotiating good terms of sale. Here are four reasons why:

1.   The vendor knows that this is a serious offer from a credit-worthy buyer.
2.   A preapproved mortgage eliminates one of the most common conditions from a sale. Many offers are conditional on a buyer securing financing. This can take several days and sometimes longer. In the meantime, the vendor has to take the home off the market, which of means, of course, that other prospective buyers will not be viewing the home. As well, in a hot real estate market, other offers can be made on the home and then you might lose out on the purchase.
3.   You can select a home and proceed with your offer knowing that the important issue of financing has been dealt with and approved in advance.
4.   With a preapproved mortgage, you are protected against any increases in interest rates for the period specified in the preapproval agreement (often 3 to 6 months). If the interest rates drop, you can still take advantage of the lower rates; but if they go up, you're protected.

The process of acquiring a prearranged mortgage is the same as applying for a mortgage after making an offer on a home. There are no drawbacks to going through the preapproval process. If you have done the GDSR and TDSR calculations earlier in this chapter, you will have taken the major steps to preapproval of your mortgage.

Appraisal The mortgage institution still has the right to refuse to provide a mortgage if the home you want to buy is not appraised at a high enough value to justify the mortgage. The mortgage institution will insist on an appraisal by an independent and qualified appraiser whom they will choose. Final approval of your mortgage is contingent on the market value of the home being high enough the qualify for the size of mortgage requested. If you're not happy with the first appraisal, it is possible to request a second one. But, as a buyer, you will be expected to pay for each appraisal (currently about $200 plus taxes).

MORTGAGE SOURCES

Lending institutions look at mortgages as attractive long-term investments with steady repayment cash flow and a guaranteed return. Because of the attractive nature of mortgages there are a large number of private lenders, special mortgage institutions, banks and credit unions who are more eager to offer mortgages to qualified buyers:

- banks
- trust companies
- finance companies
- credit unions
- life insurance companies
- mortgage brokerages
- private lenders
- parents, relatives

Before deciding to pursue a mortgage from any of the above sources ask two questions. If the vendor seems very anxious to sell, will they do a VTB mortgage at an attractive interest rate? Does the home you are considering have an assumable mortgage that you can take over? Where can you really get the best deal?

Every industry has its specialists and the mortgage industry has its own mortgage consultant, specialists and brokers. A **mortgage broker** is typically an independent with no ties to any particular lending institution and the freedom to arrange mortgages from whatever sources are best for the client. In most cases the brokers fee is paid by the lending institution with no cost to the borrower. Before committing to any mortgage from any source, it is a good idea to ask several mortgage brokers what they can do for you. This is a highly competitive business and a good mortgage broker may be able to find a mortgage at a lower interest rate and with better terms than a typical bank or lending institution will supply. Where can you find a good mortgage broker? Every real estate sales representative knows several mortgage brokers and are often more than willing to recommend one. Otherwise, you can ask the manager in the office where your real estate sales representative works.

CHAPTER SIX

Other costs in buying a home

The down payment and the mortgage are the two major costs to be considered in buying a home. However, there are other costs that must also be included in your budget. No bank or trust company will allow you to borrow the money to cover these items – you need it in cash.

Deposit Strictly speaking the deposit is not really a cost. It is part of the down payment, but you should have several thousand dollars available for your deposit before you submit an offer on a home. The usual deposit is 5% of the purchase price, payable in a certified cheque which is held in "escrow" until the deal closes. Nonetheless, the cash is out of your bank account shortly after you sign your offer to purchase.

Closing costs Closing costs will normally amount to 2% of the purchase price of the home. This percentage may vary depending on the complexity of any legal issues, the surveys required and the degree of difficulty in arranging financing.

Typical closing costs include:

- inspection fee
- legal fees
- other mortgage-related costs
- insurance
- taxes overpaid or underpaid by the vendor
- adjustments for hydro, gas or oil payments

Inspection fee Your mortgage lender may demand a house inspection or you may want an inspection for your own peace of mind. A house inspection can save you money and prevent any nasty surprises after you move in. The cost of an inspection for a $150,000 home will range from $200 to $250. The report from that inspection can be used to adjust closing costs, or determine just where and when you will have to do some work on your home.

Legal fees These will include the lawyer's time, the cost of searching your deed or land title, plus costs incurred and disbursements made on your behalf by your lawyer. Your lawyer will collect legal fees at the closing. Expect to pay from $350 to $1,000 on legal fees.

As part of earning the fee, your lawyer will do a title search to verify that the vendor has the legal right to sell the property and that there are no liens or encumbrances of any kind against the property. There is a minor charge for this as part of your lawyer's fee.

In the process of arranging for the closing, your lawyer will incur costs or disbursements for items such as couriers, registering the mortgage, title searches, drawing the title deed and long-distance phone calls. These costs will all be billed to you at the closing.

Adjustments Adjustments are made to compensate the vendor for items that they have paid for in advance. These adjustments may include items such as taxes and utilities. If taxes are due and have not been paid by the vendor, an adjustment will be made in favor of the buyer.

OTHER MORTGAGE-RELATED COSTS

Financing fees You will be expected to pay these usually small fees as part of the financing arrangements. This will be paid at the closing, by your lawyer, acting on your behalf. Ask your financial institution, ahead of time, what these fees will amount to.

Land survey fee All professional mortgage lenders will insist that there be a current survey of the property. The lender may sometimes demand a new survey to verify the boundaries of the property and confirms that there are no encroachments on your property. (An encroachment can be a neighbor's fence that is built upon your property, a driveway or even a building such as a garage or storage shed.)

Appraisal fee The lending institution will often require an independent appraisal of the property to verify its true market value. The lender must be assured that the mortgage they are underwriting does not exceed 75% of the value of the home. If it is a high-ratio mortgage, they will still want assurances as to the value of the property. You will be expected to pay the appraisal fee, which will be in the $200 range for a conventional mortgage, slightly higher for a CMHC mortgage.

Application fee Most lenders do not charge an application fee to cover the costs of processing your request for a residential mortgage, but some may do so. This can range from $100 to $200.

Mortgage broker's fee A mortgage consultant may charge a fee to arrange your financing. This fee, if any, will depend on the degree of difficulty involved in securing the best financing, at the lowest rates, with the best options to meet your requirements. Usually the fee is paid by the financial institution.

Shop around!

If you are not using a mortgage broker, always compare the rates and terms at a number of lending institutions. Your neighborhood bank may not have the best mortgage deal for you. Shop around. In some cases mortgage consultants can save you thousands of dollars by arranging financing at lower interest rates, on better terms and with longer commitment periods than most individuals are able to arrange on their own.

INSURANCE

Mortgage insurance Some lenders will insist on mortgage insurance, which protects them against the chance of your defaulting on the loan. A high ratio-mortgage lender will not advance funds without this mortgage insurance. The cost of mortgage insurance can be added to the mortgage principal. It will range from 1½-3% of the mortgage principal.

Mortgage life insurance Most mortgage lenders offer life and disability insurance. Mortgage life insurance is essentially term insurance that pays off the mortgage at the death of the borrower. Some lenders will offer this policy with the premiums being added to your monthly payment. It may seem like a good deal, but always contact an independent life insurance agent to compare costs. Often, independent term insurance can offer better prices and conditions than what your mortgage lender will put forward.

Fire and extended coverage insurance Your property is the only security your mortgage lender has for their investment. The lender will insist on proof of fire and extended coverage insurance before they will advance funds at the closing. This insurance will also cover your personal property and a living allowance to cover your costs if your property is destroyed. Ordinarily, up-front costs are small, but this will be a continuing monthly expense. Usually this "homeowner's" insurance includes a public liability section to protect you in the event that someone is injured on your property.

TAXES

Land transfer tax The land transfer tax in Canada differs from province to province. Typically it will range from 1 1/2-2% of the purchase price of the home.

GST on new homes
GST at 7% is charged on all **new** homes, condominiums and townhomes; however, a GST rebate – currently 36% – is available if the purchase price is less than $350,000 and if the home will be a primary residence and not a rental property. New homes with a purchase price in excess of $450,000 do not qualify for a GST rebate. *Check for current regulations in your province.*

There is no GST on a **resale** home. If the property has been an owner-occupied home, townhome, condominium, vacation property, cottage or apartment, there is no GST due when it is sold. If the property has been purchased and substantially renovated by a contractor who then sells it, new-home GST rules may apply depending on the extent of the renovations.

Real estate services GST must be paid on most of the real estate services listed in this section. This includes services such as the appraisal fee, the inspection fee, legal services, application fees and real estate commissions.

MOVE-IN COSTS

Move-in costs are not part of the closing costs; however, they should be budgeted for as part of your overall plan.

Moving Costs for a mover will depend on the number of rooms of furniture and the number of large heavy items such as pianos. Many young couples will move themselves with the help of friends, but there's still the expense of a rental truck and a case of beer and a pizza for your helpers.

Deposits Deposits may be required in advance for services and utilities such as telephone, gas and electricity.

Renovations You may want to make some renovations prior to moving into your new home. Sometimes defects turn up in the home inspection that can be charged back to the sellers. But most often, you'll want to tackle a paint job or put down a new floor before your furniture gets in. Plan ahead.

Double-up costs If you're doing renovations, or if you end up caught in between homes, you may face storage costs for your household goods or the doubled-up cost of a month's rent *and* a month's mortgage while work is being done. This is one more reason to keep a little reserve fund in the bank.

Your lawyer will expect a cheque to cover all these expenses, as well as the difference between your down payment and the deposit you put down on the house. Often this cheque is one of the largest you will ever write. You need to be sure, ahead of time, that you have the money needed to clear it.

Anticipating your costs

Let's anticipate some of these extra costs in three scenarios. Remember, all of these figures are estimates at the time of writing and some will vary widely depending on the property you purchase; always check for current and local figures.

Cost item	$200,000 resale home	$200,000 new home	Your scenario
Inspection fee	$250	$250 (optional)	
Legal fees	$500-800	$500-$800	
Financing fee	$0-50	$0-50	
Appraisal fee	$150	varies	
Adjustments for hydro, gas, etc.	$0-$300	none	
Mortgage consultant	$0-$150	$0-$150	
Insurance	no cash at closing	no cash at closing	
Land transfer tax	$1,000-$4,000	$1,000-$4,000	
GST on new home	$0	$10,360 (often included in purchase price)	
Real estate agent	paid by vendor	paid by vendor	
Moving	varies widely	varies widely	
Renovations	varies widely	usually none	

CHAPTER SEVEN

Closing the deal and moving in

The good news, once your offer is accepted, is that most of the hard work and the tough decisions are behind you. The bad news is that there is still a lot to do. Fortunately, most of what has to be done will be completed by other people.

The first step in the process is to get your signed offer to your lawyer immediately. Your lawyer will want to review the terms and conditions of the offer and prepare what has to be done up to and including the closing date.

After your lawyer has reviewed and approved the offer, your real estate sales representative will ask you to sign "waivers." A waiver states that a condition has been met and is no longer a part of the offer. Make arrangements with your lawyer to address any conditions of your offer. Conditions of your offer may include an inspection, appraisal and financing.

If an inspection was a condition of your offer, contact your inspector and arrange for that person to inspect the home. If the inspection company does not identify any serious problems, your real estate sales representative will prepare a waiver that removes the inspection as a condition of the offer.

If the inspection uncovers major items, you should review the written report with your real estate sales representative immediately. You can often walk away from the house deal at this point and get your deposit back. Alternatively, you can reopen negotiations to address the problem, usually by getting the vendor to pay for fixing the problem uncovered by the inspectors.

If financing was a condition of your offer, you must move quickly to find or confirm your mortgage arrangements. The mortgage lender will require an independent appraisal of the property. Normally the lender will make arrangements and schedule the appraisal. As soon as your financing is firm, your real estate sales representative will ask you to sign another waiver that removes financing as a condition of the offer.

This is a sample waiver. It is used to verify that any conditions of the offer have been waived (settled to your satisfaction).

WAIVER

I/WE, the undersigned Purchaser/Lessee/Vendor/Lessor of property known as:

_____ hereby waive the following condition(s):

as set out in an Agreement of Purchase and Sale/Offer to Lease,

dated _____, 19___

between _____
as Purchaser/Lessee

and _____
as Vendor/Lessor.

I / We will proceed with the purchase/lease of the above-mentioned property. All terms and conditions of the said Agreement of Purchase and Sale/Offer to Lease will remain the same, and shall be deemed to be firm and binding upon the parties hereto.

Dated at _____ this _____ day of _____, 19___

_____   _____   _____
(Witness)   (Purchaser/Lessee/Vendor/Lessor)   (Date)

_____   _____   _____
(Witness)   (Purchaser/Lessee/Vendor/Lessor)   (Date)

LEGAL CONCERNS

Once the conditions of your offer have been addressed, your lawyer will initiate the legal prerequisites that must be completed at the closing. In addition to addressing all the legal issues on your behalf, your lawyer will co-ordinate delivery of your mortgage funds from your lender and arrange the closing details with the vendor's lawyer.

Your lawyer will have a large number of activities to address prior to and in preparation for the closing. These activities include the following:

- verifying that all conditions have been met by receipt of waivers
- acquiring a copy of the land survey or arrange for one to be made, which must, in most circumstances, show all existing dwellings
- transferring or buying insurance coverage for your home upon closing
- arranging a title search to verify that the vendor has title (legal ownership) and is able to convey valid title
- confirming that there are no liens or encumbrances against the property (for instance, if renovations were done by a contractor who wasn't paid in full) and if there are, making sure they will be discharged and vacated at closing
- ensuring that the property has no violations of the building code
- checking that the property has no violations of zoning restrictions/work orders
- verifying that all taxes are paid on the property
- inquiring with utility companies to ensure there are no existing arrears
- calculating the land transfer tax and the GST due
- reviewing the financing arrangements
- arranging for the transfer of funds at the close
- reviewing all legal documentation with respect to completing the transaction
- co-ordinating the closing with the vendor's lawyer

It is always a good idea to stay in contact with your lawyer and your mortgage lender to be sure that everything is proceeding according to plan and will be ready for the closing day. Your lawyer will ask you to sign all the legal documents a day or two prior to the closing. In most cases, there will be no need for you to be at the closing itself. You may never meet the seller of the house unless you make a special effort to do so.

After the closing, your lawyer will turn over the keys to you along with, in due course, copies of all the legal documentation and a full accounting of the funds disbursed in a comprehensive reporting letter. At the same time, the lawyer will want your cheque to cover her fees, costs and the difference between the mortgage and whatever money you put down in your deposit.

CLOSING DAY COSTS

You can use this form to estimate the costs you'll have to cover on closing day.

Item	Typical ($)	Your estimate
Obtaining abstract of title (approx.)*	$100	
Sheriff's certificates ($11/name) approx.	45	
Subdivision compliance	55	
Tax certificate	25	
Certificate of zoning, building, setbacks, compliance	80	
Hydro inquiry	7	
Water inquiry	20	
Consumers gas inquiry	12	
Hydro easement	30	
Registration of deed	50	
Registration of mortgage	50	
Where applicable, septic tank inquiry, re: user permit, well function and environment assessment, if in concession lot	75	
Where applicable, swimming pool, cabana inquiry, re: fences, locks, compliance with municipal by-laws	80	
Estimated total	**629**	

* Searches vary if property is in land titles or registry system.

Plus land transfer tax (based on purchase price). This varies by locality.

MOVING TO YOUR NEW HOUSE

Sometimes you might want to schedule a personal meeting with the current owners of a resale house. This would give you a chance to find out, after the sale, some of the fine points that might not have been discussed beforehand. How often does the furnace fan need oiling? Do the next-door-neighbors party every Friday or only once a year? There are nitty-gritty details about the operation of any house, and the current owners know them best.

If you've bought a new home, you'll want to know when the builder expects to have it finished or when you can conceivably move in. The builder's sales representative will be helpful on these items, though it's always wise to anticipate delays on unfinished houses in new subdivisions.

Either on closing day or shortly thereafter, you'll face the task of moving into your new home. Without a doubt, professional movers are the easiest way to make this move – but they may cost from several hundred to several thousand dollars. If you can afford it, or if your company is helping out, professional movers will look after every aspect of your move: planning, packing, moving and unpacking. They'll cover any damage and advise you on what items you really should move yourself (the antique crystal, a favorite houseplant).

For young couples just starting off, moving is more often done with a rental van and a gang of friends to help out. Remember that rental vans are cheapest mid-week and mid-month, but that your friends may not be available on those days. If you're moving within the same area, you might be able to do the move in stages, a few boxes at a time, and then finish up with the big items.

Preparing your current home for sale

There is more to selling a home than setting a price and calling up an agent. While a good price obviously is a major consideration, and quite essential if you want to move on to another home, it's wise to think through the other important factors:

- selling your house at the highest price the market will bear
- selling your house as quickly as possible (or exactly when you want to)
- selling your house on your terms

The best way to achieve these objectives is to have a good real estate agent to represent you. A good agent will help you determine a price, advise you on fixing up your home for showing and work through the entire process of the sale - including negotiations with prospective buyers - with you. When your house sells, the agent and the real estate firm will pick up a hefty fee from you (4-6% of the selling price), but they do earn their money. And remember, only a quarter to a third of that fee goes directly to the agent, the rest is for advertising, overhead and the real estate company.

Often real estate agents want to start selling your home with an "exclusive listing." This means that your agent, and only your agent, is acting on your behalf to sell the house. The advantage of this arrangement to the agent is obvious - he or she gets a full fee, or half the split fee if the buyer is smart enough to have an agent. The advantage to you is that you have your agent's full attention. He or she is as motivated to sell your house as you are.

A good agent will work with you on the key items:

- setting an appropriate asking price
- developing a listing and feature sheet for your house that emphasizes its strong features
- scheduling an agent's inspection and the first open house days
- setting up your home so it "shows" well

If your home does not sell within a month or so, your listing ordinarily goes to the local MLS (Multiple Listing Service). This places your listing in the hands of every realtor in the area – and theoretically brings it to the attention of many more buyers. At this point, your agent must share the fee with the final selling agent and the buyer's agent, so a few may be reluctant to move quickly to the MLS listing. Nonetheless, if an exclusive listing doesn't produce results, an MLS listing might be what you need to sell your home.

The price that you select for your home will have a direct impact on the number of qualified buyers who will visit your home. The objective is to have the maximum number of qualified buyers so that you can generate the maximum number of offers. In the final analysis, you can get a better price for your home if it is priced realistically. A good real estate agent will give you a solid estimate of the price you'll probably get and give you advice on the asking

The best agent for you

The *best* agent to sell your home:

- has had many successful listings in your neighborhood
- gives you a fair evaluation of what price you should ask for your house
- gets along well with you and your partner

The *best* agent isn't always a friend, or the agent who sold you the house, or the one with the lowest commission or the one who suggests the highest listing price. The *best* agent for you is one who is honest in evaluating your property, who has a track record of success and whom you can trust in tough negotiations.

price you should set. But don't choose your agent on the basis of wild estimations of your home's worth. Some agents will suggest an inflated figure in order to get your business; then you'll have to chop the asking price later in order to get any offers. An honest evaluation at the start will save you time and grief in the selling process.

DETERMINING A SELLING PRICE

The correct selling price is the highest price the market will bear. There are three factors that will assist you in deciding the correct selling price of your home:

- the price of similar homes that have sold in the last six months
- the price of similar homes that are for sale now
- information from listings that have expired in the last six months.

The final selling price of similar homes recently purchased in your neighborhood is always the best indicator of how much buyers are prepared to spend for your home. In addition, expired listings provide valuable information on what price ranges did not work. In many cases, listings expire and the home is taken off the market because the price was set too high. This at least gives you an indication of what's too much to ask for your home.

Ask your real estate agent to fill in the following forms for all three categories and to show you the backup information.

The key to making this a valid exercise is to be sure that you are comparing your home to similar homes. In the first column, on the left, fill in the major features of your home. These should be major features such as how many bedrooms, finished basement, den, family room, walkout basement, double or single-car garage and total floor plan size. The homes your real estate agent adds to the other columns must be comparable to yours.

You will not need to be a genius to see that if comparable homes are selling for $150,000, you will not be able to sell your home for $175,000 no matter how much you love it or how much money you put into that fancy new brick driveway.

SOLD IN THE LAST SIX MONTHS

This analysis of comparable homes in the neighborhood is an important guideline because it tells you:

- what homes were on the market
- at what price
- for how many days
- what they actually sold for

Your home	Comparable home 1	Comparable home 2	Comparable home 3	Comparable home 4	Comparable home 5
Size					
Feature 2					
Feature 3					
Feature 4					
Feature 5					
Notes					
List price					
Days on market					
Selling price					

FOR SALE NOW

This analysis of comparable homes gives you a clear picture of the competition. If the home down the street listed at $150,000 has the same floor space, the same number of bedrooms and is in the same condition as your home, it is unrealistic to imagine that a buyer will spend $175,000 for your home. If you were a buyer, would you? This analysis shows you:

• what homes are on the market
• at what prices
• how many days the homes have been listed
• what the original asking price was

Your home	Comparable home 1	Comparable home 2	Comparable home 3	Comparable home 4	Comparable home 5
Size					
Feature 2					
Feature 3					
Feature 4					
Feature 5					
Notes					
List price					
Days on market					

EXPIRED IN THE LAST SIX MONTHS – TAKEN OFF THE MARKET

An analysis of expired listings is an analysis of what price ranges *did not work* for comparable homes in the neighborhood. This analysis shows you:

- what homes did not sell
- what prices did not work
- for how many days the home was listed

Your home	Comparable home 1	Comparable home 2	Comparable home 3	Comparable home 4	Comparable home 5
Size					
Feature 2					
Feature 3					
Feature 4					
Feature 5					
Notes					
List price					
Days on market					

Most homeowners believe that their house is special and that its true market value is higher that it really is. This is to be expected. We become familiar with our home and our neighborhood. We hear stories about how much someone else sold their home for. We really think that our decorating and renovations are exactly what someone else will love. And some real estate sales agents will play into our fantasies by accepting a listing at what they know is an unrealistic price just to get the business.

But what happens when your home is placed on the market at a price well above its true market value?

1. There is less activity than there should be and very few reasonable offers.
2. The listing agent will ultimately suggest a price reduction which you will be forced to accept very reluctantly.
3. At some point, your for sale sign will say "Price just reduced." As a buyer, wouldn't this make you wonder what is wrong with the property?
4. If there are still no reasonable offers the agent may recommend one more price reduction "to adjust for today's tough market."
5. Now that the house is correctly priced, it faces another serious problem. Real estate agents wonder why the house was on the market for so long and why it had so many price reductions. Their assumption is that something must be wrong with the property and it does not get the attention or the showings that it deserves.

At some point in time, a buyer will offer a price well below the market value of your home. The buyer knows that the home has been listed for a long time with several price reductions. He or she can use this information to justify the lower price. By this point in time, you may be so discouraged with the process that you might accept the lousy offer.

All this can be avoided by pricing your home reasonably at the outset.

PACKAGING YOUR HOME TO SELL

The next challenge, after setting a price, is to package your home to sell, just as you would package any product in order to present its best possible image. Imagine the care that jewellers take to present their products, particularly their most expensive product, in the best possible way. You must take the same approach to packaging your home so that it is presented in the best possible light.

Remember that the first impression is vital. You want every view of your home to create that "instantaneous, positive first impression." You only get one chance to create it.

In the world of marketing and advertising, it is common knowledge that "perception is reality." Your home must be perceived by the buyer as a well-kept home that will make a good home for their family. Only then will potential buyers give it serious consideration.

A positive first impression should lead the buyer to thinking:

- "This home is well kept."
- "I could move into this home tomorrow with no hassles."
- "I could be very comfortable in this home."

Buyers must be able to picture themselves living in the home, eating in the kitchen, watching television in the family room, entertaining friends in the living room and being proud of their new home.

How do you create a positive first impression? The following four points will help set the stage to sell your home:

- Be objective
- NCR: Neat – Clean – Repaired
- Nothing scary
- Dramatize and neutralize

Be objective You have probably become so accustomed to your home that being objective can be tough. Everything is where you want it to be and it is very comfortable. Now you must look at your house objectively, just as if you were looking at it for the first time through the eyes of a buyer.

One of the best ways to evaluate the appearance of your home is to visit several open houses and compare the appearance of your home to them.

The appearance of your home and how well it shows can result in the following advantages:

- a substantial difference in the selling price
- a major impact on how fast it sells
- an increase in exposure by other real estate agents

Sometimes a friend or real estate agent can help you see more clearly. That wonderful lime-green paint that you selected with such care … well, maybe it looks a little strange to others. The cluttered front hall … perhaps it would look better if some of the junk were put away. Your children's magic-marker scribbles on the wall are so charming to you – but these will be off-putting to a buyer.

You have to look at your home with fresh eyes, compare it to other houses, and then make the cosmetic changes necessary to show your home to advantage. Use the checklists in chapter 9 to help.

NCR The next step in creating a positive first impression is NCR: Neat – Clean – Repaired. As you step through your home from the driveway to the bedrooms, remember that key phrase NCR.

Neat means that your home is not cluttered. There are no magazines lying around. All the toys have been put away. All the clothes are in closets and there are no dishes in the sink. These may seem to be very small items but any clutter creates an immediate negative impression.

Neat means that you may have to take a few items of furniture and store them elsewhere until your home is sold. Your great big "Lazyboy" is so comfortable but it looks well past its prime. Your large free-standing cupboard in the kitchen is practical, but takes up too much room. These may be familiar, useful and comfortable items but if they take up a lot of space or detract from the neat appearance of a room, they should be stored somewhere else.

Neat means that you may have to take down some pictures or photographs if they make the walls look too busy. Sooner or later you will have to pack everything. Why not pack as many items as possible early, so that your home looks completely uncluttered? As you step through each room and look in each closet, ask yourself if you could pack these items or store them elsewhere.

Clean means that every counter top, every window, every floor sparkles. Clean means more than appearance, it also includes smell. If you have pets, be sure that pet smells have been neutralized. Many of the buyers who walk through your home will be either allergic to animals or afraid of pets. Any pet smells will create a negative impression. It may be a good idea to bring in a professional cleaning crew to give your home a complete cleaning from top to bottom – *before* you list your house.

Repaired is a reminder to fix any item that creates an impression of neglect no matter how small it may be. A dripping faucet, a cracked window, any peeling paint must be fixed. Even a small item that is broken sends a subtle message that the owners of this home have neglected to maintain it. This suggests that there may be some major items in need of repair.

Nothing scary Scary items are those that create an impression of a lack of care or serious structural problems. Paint peeling from a ceiling, a light that doesn't work, a stiff door or cracks in a wall that suggest shifting foundations, water stains that hint at bad plumbing – all are scary items. They create an immediate negative first impression. Walk through your home with your agent to look for items that may have been overlooked.

Dramatize and neutralize To dramatize is to select unique items and build on them. To neutralize is to take negative items and minimize their impact. You'll want to dramatize items such as fireplaces, picture windows, hardwood floors, curved stairs and large bright kitchens. These are impressive selling features and should be played up as much as possible.

Items such as brass fireplace utensils should be displayed beside the fireplace to draw attention to it. Logs should be in a neat woodpile beside the fireplace. Hardwood floors should be highly polished with small throw rugs that draw attention to the floors. The curtains on a picture window should be drawn back so that the window and the view capture the buyer's attention. Select the most impressive features of your home and arrange furniture and accessories to dramatize their appeal.

Neutralize means to downplay the eccentric items of your home. When you painted the house, you may have selected those bright green cupboard doors. But, that was five years ago and today that bright green may be considered garish. As you walk though your home, your agent will point out items that may overwhelm a room or create a negative impression. In most cases, you will be able to avoid major costs to neutralize a negative feature. In some cases, it may be well worth an investment to repaint or even replace items that will create a negative impression.

REVIEW YOUR HOME BEFORE THE "FOR SALE" SIGN GOES UP

The next chapter provides a series of checklists to guide you in preparing your home for sale. These will help in the three house reviews that are essential before a strong sale.

First review The first review occurs when you start at the bottom of your driveway and go through every room in your home to identify any major items that you will remove or repair.

Second review This is your "packaging" review. As you go through the checklists, you will be packaging every room for sale. There may be more than one of these "second" reviews to keep your home properly packaged.

Third review The third is the "presentation" review. In this review, you will be taking steps to dramatize every room to create that positive first impression. This presentation review takes place as you prepare the home for an open house or for a showing.

Remember, real estate agents often add flowers, bring in furniture, turn on radios and even spray fragrance to make a house appealing. You might want to consider all of these, but only after you've done the serious work your house may need.

Photo tips

The following suggestions have been provided to ensure that your Multiple Listing Service pictures are of high quality:

1. Please remember that a photo will be taken on the same day the contract is received at the relevant real estate board.
2. Ensure that there are no renovations taking place on the exterior of the building.
3. Keep the garage door closed and cars out of the driveway on the day the photo is being taken.
4. Keep all garbage out of the way, even if it's garbage collection day.
5. Maintain the exterior – mow the lawn in summer and shovel the driveway in the winter.

BEFORE AN OPEN HOUSE

These are the finishing touches to be made just before an open house or just before a buyer arrives to be shown through your home.

Driveway
If at all possible there should be no more than one car in the driveway. The ideal is no cars at all in the driveway.

Front door and entrance
Place a large plant, possibly a hanging plant, near the front door. Hang a wreath on the door.
Place a welcome mat in front of the door.

Living room
Place a large vase of flowers on a coffee table in the center of the living room.
Have lights focused on pictures.

Family room

Be sure that the fireplace accessories are in place with a neat pile of fireplace logs close by. If possible have a fire burning in the fireplace.

Throw an afghan over a chair to enhance the feeling of warmth and comfort.

Have a game neatly laid out on a coffee table.

Kitchen

Be sure that all the lights are on and that the kitchen is bright. During the day, the blinds should be open.

Place a vase of flowers or a plant on the kitchen table.

Have freshly baked cookies sitting on the counter.

Dining room

Arrange items on the dining room table to dramatize the feeling of fine dining. For instance, a silver tea set on a buffet in the dining room creates an image of elegance.

Downstairs bathroom

Be sure that your "show" towels are in place.

Have a scented candle burning.

Have scented soap on the sink.

Have a set of matching bathroom glass and soap holder.

Front closet

The best way to dramatize a closet is to be sure that it is only one-half to three-quarters full and that the floor and shelves are neat.

Master bedroom

Arrange your best bedspread with matching pillowcases on the bed.

Be sure that lights beside the bed are on.

Have an open book on the night table.

Other bedrooms

Arrange toys to present an image of comfort.

Use your best bedspreads on the beds.

Arrange decorative pillows on the beds.

Upstairs bathrooms
Use show towels.
Use scented candles and scented soap.

Basement
Have a project or hobby in place on a workbench.

Garage
All tools should be stored neatly to dramatize the usefulness of
the garage.

Recreation room
Have one or two toys or games strategically placed to demonstrate the fun aspects of the room.

Den
Have one book on the desk with a bookmark in it.

APPOINTMENTS AND ADVERTISING

The appointment process is important to understand as it is
another step towards selling your home. Good agents will inspect
a home before showing it to a client to prevent everyone from
wasting time. Agent "open house" days are for the purpose of
inspection; however, it is sometimes impossible for every agent to
inspect every home.

Showings involve bringing a potential buyer through your
home. To set up either an agent inspection or a client showing, an
appointment should be made in advance so the homeowner has
some advance warning. It's always best to be "away somewhere"
when an agent is showing your home to a potential buyer.

Why the "for sale" sign? While many individuals would prefer
not to have a "for sale" sign on the front lawn, there is a 20% chance
your home will sell as a direct result of someone seeing the sign
and calling your agent or co-operating agents.

If you are worried about the neighbors knowing your home
is for sale, don't be. They will know soon enough just by seeing the
great number of strangers coming to your door. Quite often neighbors have friends or relatives who would like to live in the same
neighborhood. They can be your best advertising – but only when
they know you're intending to sell.

Lockbox A lockbox provides convenient access to your home for selling agents. This is an important item as it allow them to bring more potential buyers through your home. An agent doesn't want to be burdened with picking up numerous keys, remembering which key is for which door and potentially losing them. The lockbox avoids this problem.

Showing tips When an appointment is made to show your home, you can make sure it looks its best by taking a few steps before you go out:

- **Turn on all lights.** This is an absolute must whenever showings occur. Darkness portrays a dullness and creates an atmosphere that may lead to potential buyers imagining that you are hiding your home's flaws. Light creates a positive mood, which creates good feelings. Positive impressions of your home will lead to a quick sale.
- **Turn on the stereo.** This background noise makes for a pleasant atmosphere and may also mask noise from the neighbors or a baseball game at a nearby park.
- **Bake something or make coffee.** Store merchandisers know that the smell of baking cookies or brewing coffee puts customers into a mood to buy.
- **Don't be home when buyers come in.** People who spend thousands of dollars buying what usually is their biggest investment want to feel at ease when inspecting your home. When you are in the house, the buyers will not talk freely with their agent, nor will they look as hard at the special features your home has to offer. They feel as if they are intruders.

Studies show that buyers walk through a home three times faster when the seller is at home. You want the prospective buyers to take their time, to feel comfortable and at home, to imagine themselves living in the home, to picture *their* furniture in every room. For that to happen, go out and have coffee with a friend when buyers come to call.

SELLING YOUR OWN HOME

Every year, a small number of homeowners decide to sell their homes by themselves, without the help of an agent or a real estate firm. Why? The advantage is price: you can save thousands of dollars compared to the fee an agent will charge.

There are disadvantages, however. In handling your own sale, you are responsible for every detail from preparing the house, to advertising, to negotiating the final agreement. You have to put up with the inconvenience of arranging your own showings, looking after your own open house and dealing with many people who may or may not be serious about buying your home. For most people selling their own homes, the inconvenience and time wasted outweigh any financial savings. But if you want to sell your house yourself, there are do-it-yourself kits available for a few hundred dollars that come complete with instructions, forms and even a "for sale" sign. If you do decide to go ahead and sell your own home, these are the steps to follow.

Prepare your home. We've already explained the NCR approach to preparing your home for sale. Since there will be no agent to advise you, it's best to have a friend or relative do a "walk through" inspection of your house acting as a prospective buyer. The feedback you receive will help you get your house ready for sale. The checklists in the next chapter will also assist you.

Assemble the information you'll need for prospective buyers and the home fact sheet. Get the latest figures for taxes, hydro and heating costs. If your mortgage is going to be assumed or blended, get current details on principal and monthly payments. Have a photographer take a picture of your house that accentuates its best features. Some homeowners even have a production team make a video of the home, with shots taken inside and out, so prospective buyers can tour your home a second time on their televisions.

Set a price and a time frame. You can use the forms on pages 82 to 84 to help establish your own asking price for your home. The most frequent problem for people selling their own homes comes from setting an unrealistic price. Your home undoubtedly has a special charm and attractiveness for you that a prospective buyer will not fully appreciate, so your price must ultimately reflect the *real estate value* of your home, not its *emotional value* to you. Friends and neighbors who can speak candidly with you will let you know if your asking price is reasonable. Another handy rule is "If you don't get 25 calls in the first week, your price is too high." If those calls don't come in, then you'll end up in the unenviable position of having to offer your house "price reduced." Best to set the asking price properly at the outset.

In most cases, you won't want to wait forever to sell your home. Set a realistic timeline – two months or, at most, six months. Be prepared to adjust your advertising and asking price until your house gets some attention from prospective buyers. Remember, you're not a real estate professional, so you'll make some mistakes along the way. But don't let the selling process drag on indefinitely.

Arrange for professional help now – for later on. When the deal to sell is finally agreed upon, you'll need some professional help right away. You'll want to have a lawyer look through the agreement (even if you use a preprinted form from the local real estate board) to make sure you're protected. You'll also need to have someone hold the deposit in escrow until the deal is closed. As well, it will be helpful if your mortgage lender is ready for the sale, if you have a home inspection company ready to go and if you have the name of a mortgage broker. Try to arrange all this ahead of time.

Advertise. When you're got everything else in place, it's time to begin advertising. Advertising, of course, comes in many forms. At the very least, you'll have to prepare and pay for a **newspaper advertisement**. Costs can range from as low as $50 for a few weekend placements of a print ad in a community newspaper to several thousand dollars for a large advertisement with a photograph in a national newspaper. Often you'll have to place the same ad in a number of different publications.

Your newspaper ad should look like those placed by professional realtors: a catchy headline, a brief description of the home highlights, an "asking" price to show you're willing to bargain, the date for your first open house and some phrase like "just on the market" or "won't last" to give potential buyers a sense that they should hurry to view your home.

The newspaper advertisement is actually a smaller version of the **fact sheet** on your home. Your fact sheet can use an entire sheet of paper, or two, to outline the key selling points of your house and provide photographs of the house and its features. The fact sheet can be given to people who visit your home or drop in to the open house.

Some communities also have a **cable television** station that features homes for sale. You'll have to seek out details on costs and visual requirements if you want to use this service. As well, you might want to put up an **Internet** site about your house. Sometimes such a site can be linked to community Internet listings so a potential buyer on the other side of the country can do an Internet tour of many homes for sale in your area, including yours. You'll need photographs and the information from your fact sheet to set up the site, and you might want to arrange for some computer help to make sure the site is as attractive as possible.

Even in our technological age, **word of mouth** is still a valuable way to let prospective buyers know that your home is for sale. You should tell your family and neighbors about the sale, post a notice at work, stick up a small flyer at the local butcher shop or supermarket. You'll also have to put up a **sign** on your lawn to let drive-by potential homebuyers know that your house is for sale. It's possible to do one yourself with a paintbrush and stencils, but a professionally made sign will look better and convey the message that you're serious about selling the house.

Stage an open house. After you've prepared your house and run an ad announcing the event, it's time for the first open house. You'll have to act as greeter, real estate agent and homeowner – all at once. Be prepared for neighbors, competing homesellers and the merely curious to walk across your doorstep. You have to put up with all of these people so the handful of serious prospective buyers can have a chance to get their first look at your home.

The first open house rarely results in a sale, but it could lead to potential buyers who return for a showing – either on their own or with an agent. Ordinarily, you'll want to wait two weeks or so before doing a second open house. A house that is perpetually "open" gives the impression that you are quite desperate to sell it – obviously not an impression that leads to effective negotiations.

Show your house. Both before and after the open house, you must be ready to "show" your home to potential buyers. This involves giving the potential buyers and their agents a fact sheet, a brief sales pitch (no more than a minute or two) and a quick tour through your home. The more serious buyers will probably want to go through the house again, on their own or with their agent. As we mentioned in chapter 3, buyers often do three visits and may do five or more before they decide to put in an offer.

It's usually best to schedule house showings so that you're doing several potential buyers at a time. This gives the impression that there's a great deal of interest in your house. It also makes it less onerous to get the house cleaned and ready for inspection by potential buyers. See the next chapter for more on this.

Consider offers and counter-offers. When an offer to purchase is made on your home, you must act as both vendor and agent. This means you must look after your interests as the seller and also try to work out a deal that will permit the purchase to take place. Wearing two hats, like this, is not an easy business. It is possible, at this point, to ask your lawyer to negotiate on your behalf and act as the go-between for offers and counter-offers. The fees for this can be considerable, so be prepared.

Or you can negotiate yourself. You really didn't expect to get your full asking price, did you? So how far down are you prepared to settle? And what conditions can you live with? You should think through the various financing options and possible conditions on the sale before you're in the midst of negotiations. (Review chapter 4 for more on this.)

Complete the deal. Don't do it yourself. This is where a lawyer is essential. While you might be an excellent person to prepare your house, advertise its sale and negotiate terms, there's too much money at stake to risk hundreds of thousands of dollars at the close. Even lawyers usually get *other* lawyers to handle a house closing. That way, if anything goes wrong, there's insurance for legal errors.

CHAPTER NINE

Checklists for selling your home

Driveway (curb appeal)

As strange as it may sound, it is estimated that over half of all homes are sold before the buyers get out of their car. Every buying decision is an emotional decision, even if logic is used to justify the eventual purchase. This is the best example of the importance of making a positive first impression. Spend 10 minutes looking at your home from the bottom of your driveway, from the curb side and from across the street. Walk slowly up your driveway and look at your home through the eyes of a buyer who is seeing the home for the very first time. Does your home have "curb appeal"? Does the home present a neat appearance? Does it look as if it received tender love and care? Does it look inviting? Will it look like "home" to a buyer?

Driveway

NEAT	
Bushes trimmed	
Flowers appropriately located	
No signs of pet activity	
CLEAN	
Driveway	
Front walk and steps	
Windows	
Trim	

REPAIRED	
Driveway	
Front walk and steps	
Windows	
Peeling paint	
DRAMATIZE	
Brass house numbers	
Brass door fixture	
Large plant near front steps	
Hanging flowers	
NEUTRALIZE	
Any negative features	

Front door and entranceway

Imagine that you are a buyer and you are walking through your front door for the very first time. What is your first impression of this home? How does it look? How does it feel? How does it smell? How does it sound?

With a little extra care, entrance stairs can present a very positive image. The best approach is to dramatize them with flowers, ornaments or something welcoming.

Front door and entrance way

NEAT	
Remove any clutter	
Remove any extra furniture	
CLEAN	
Carpet, spot or full clean	
Furniture	
Lighting fixtures	
Hardwood floors, wood trim	
REPAIRED	
Cracks in wall, ceiling	
Paint, wallpaper	
DRAMATIZE	
Brass house numbers, door	
Fixtures	
Brighter lights	
Large flower display	
Large mirror	
NEUTRALIZE	
Light paint color	
Neutral wallpaper	

Stairs

NEAT	
Be sure that there is absolutely nothing on the stairs that a buyer could trip over	
Remove any extra items	
CLEAN	
Carpet, spot or full clean	
Hardwood floors, banisters – shine	
Lighting to highlight the stairs	
REPAIRED	
Any broken railings	
Any worn or torn carpet	
Paint, wallpaper	
DRAMATIZE	
Brighter lights	
Large mirror	
NEUTRALIZE	
Light paint color	
Neutral wallpaper	

Living room and family room

In most homes, the living room is the first room that a buyer sees. The living room is the showpiece of your home. Make it neat and attractive, emphasizing its most "homey" features. In most homes, the family room is the real living room. The family room becomes the center of activity for most families, so it should suggest purposeful activity. The family room and the kitchen are the two most important rooms in the home in terms of buyers seeing this as "their" home.

Living room

NEAT	
Remove magazines, newspapers	
Arrange furniture to create an open feeling	
Remove extra plants, furniture	
CLEAN	
Carpet, spot or full clean	
Hardwood floors – shine	
Drapes, curtains, blinds	
Lighting fixtures	
REPAIRED	
Cracks in wall, ceiling	
Paint, wallpaper	
DRAMATIZE	
Brighter lights	
Large flower display	
Large mirror	
NEUTRALIZE	
Light paint color	
Neutral wallpaper	

Family room

NEAT	
Remove magazines, newspapers	
Arrange furniture to create an open feeling	
Remove extra plants, furniture	
CLEAN	
Carpet, spot or full clean	
Hardwood floors – shine	
Drapes, curtains, blinds	
Lighting fixtures	
REPAIRED	
Cracks in wall, ceiling	
Paint, wallpaper	
DRAMATIZE	
Brighter lights	
Large flower display	
Large mirror	
NEUTRALIZE	
Light paint color	
Neutral wallpaper	

Kitchen and dining room

In most homes, the dining room is a show piece used infrequently and only for special occasions. Most buyers will give the dining room a quick glance and a walk through. It may not be as important as the kitchen or family room, but it must have a positive impact that encourages buyers to envision having their holiday dinners there.

Kitchen	
NEAT	
Counters – remove and store extra appliances	
Cupboards – remove and store extra food, utensils	
Remove extra plants, furniture, fixtures	
Hide magazines, newspapers, etc.	
CLEAN	
Floors – spotless and shining	
Cupboards – spotless in and out	
Sinks and counter area	
Appliances and vents	
Garbage area – clean and deodorize	
Walls	
Curtains, blinds	
Lighting fixtures	
REPAIRED	
Cracks in wall, ceiling	
Leaking faucets	
Paint, wallpaper	
DRAMATIZE	
Brighter lights	
Large flower display	
Large mirror	
NEUTRALIZE	
Light paint color	
Neutral wallpaper	

Dining room	
NEAT	
Remove magazines, newspapers, books, etc.	
Arrange furniture to create an open feeling	
Remove extra plants, furniture, fixtures	
CLEAN	
Carpet, spot or full clean	
Hardwood floors – shine	
Drapes, curtains, blinds	
Lighting fixtures	
REPAIRED	
Cracks in wall, ceiling	
Paint, wallpaper	
DRAMATIZE	
Brighter lights	
Large flower display	
Large mirror	
Linens on table	
Silver set on serving tray	
NEUTRALIZE	
Light paint color	
Neutral wallpaper	

Master bathroom and downstairs bathroom

Take a little extra care with the master bathroom. It will be viewed by the buyer as an extension of the master bedroom and given the same degree of consideration.

Downstairs bathroom

NEAT	
Remove magazines, newspapers, books, etc.	
Remove extra accessories	
Medicine cabinets – remove and store all non-essentials	
Linen closets – remove and store all non-essentials	
CLEAN	
Sinks, tub, shower, faucets, toilet	
Floor and walls – clean, deodorize	
Curtains, blinds	
Mirrors, lighting fixtures	
REPAIRED	
Cracks in wall, ceiling, tiles	
Toilets and plumbing	
Caulking around sinks, tubs	
Paint, wallpaper	
DRAMATIZE	
Brighter lights	
Flower display	
Large mirror	
Show towels, accessories	
Scented soaps, candles	
NEUTRALIZE	
Light paint color	
Neutral wallpaper	

Master bathroom

NEAT	
Remove magazines, newspapers, books, etc.	
Remove extra accessories	
Medicine cabinets – remove and store all non-essentials	
Linen closets – remove and store all non-essentials	
CLEAN	
Sinks, tub, shower, faucets, toilet	
Floor and walls – clean, deodorize	
Curtains, blinds	
Mirrors, lighting fixtures	
REPAIRED	
Cracks in wall, ceiling, tiles	
Toilets and plumbing	
Caulking around sinks, tubs	
Paint, wallpaper	
DRAMATIZE	
Brighter lights	
Flower display	
Large mirror	
Show towels, accessories	
Scented soaps, candles	
NEUTRALIZE	
Light paint color	
Neutral wallpaper	

Master bedroom and other bedrooms

The master bedroom is one of the three most important rooms in a home for most buyers. We spend one-third of our lives sleeping and we look for a safe, comfortable haven. The master bedroom is where we keep many of our valuable and personal items including clothes and jewelry.

All other bedrooms must also project an image of warmth and comfort.

Master bedroom

NEAT	
Remove magazines, newspapers, books, etc.	
Arrange furniture to create an open feeling	
Remove extra plants, furniture	
Remove non-essential items	
CLEAN	
Carpet, spot or full clean	
Hardwood floors – shine	
Drapes, curtains, blinds	
Lighting fixtures	
REPAIRED	
Cracks in wall, ceiling	
Paint, wallpaper	
DRAMATIZE	
Add curtains or valances	
NEUTRALIZE	
Warm, light paint color	
Neutral wallpaper	

Other bedrooms

NEAT	
Remove magazines, newspapers, books, etc.	
Arrange furniture to create an open feeling	
Remove extra plants, furniture	
Remove non-essential items	
CLEAN	
Carpet, spot or full clean	
Hardwood floors – shine	
Drapes, curtains, blinds	
Lighting fixtures	
REPAIRED	
Cracks in wall, ceiling	
Paint, wallpaper	
DRAMATIZE	
Add curtains or valances	
NEUTRALIZE	
Warm, light paint color	
Neutral wallpaper	

Upstairs bathroom and closets

Closets that are jammed look smaller. They make it difficult for buyers to picture their clothes hanging in that closet. Well-organized closets, that are not quite full, reinforce a positive first impression. It says that the occupants of this home take good care of things. Therefore, they must have taken good care of the rest of their home.

Upstairs bathroom

NEAT	
Remove magazines, newspapers, books, etc.	
Remove extra accessories	
Medicine cabinets – remove and store all non-essentials	
Linen closets – remove and store all non-essentials	
CLEAN	
Sinks, tub, shower, faucets, toilet	
Floor and walls – clean, deodorize	
Curtains, blinds	
Mirrors, lighting fixtures	
REPAIRED	
Cracks in wall, ceiling, tiles	
Toilets and plumbing	
Caulking around sinks, tubs	
Paint, wallpaper	
DRAMATIZE	
Brighter lights	
Flower display	
Large mirror	
Show towels, accessories	
Scented soaps, candles	
NEUTRALIZE	
Light paint color	
Neutral wallpaper	

Closets

NEAT	
Remove and store all non-essential items	
Straighten clothes on hangers, have all articles facing the same way	
Straighten shoes and other items on floor	
CLEAN	
Doors, mirrors	
Floor and walls	
REPAIRED	
Cracks in wall, ceiling, tiles	
Shelves, hooks	
Paint	

Basement and garage

The impression of a small garage can be minimized by having nothing in the garage except one car with no lawnmowers and gardening tools to create clutter.

Basement

NEAT	
Store all non-essential items	
Remove magazines, newspapers, loose papers	
CLEAN	
Floors – sweep clean	
Sinks and laundry areas	
Walls dusted	
Lighting fixtures	
REPAIRED	
Cracks in wall, basement floor	
Leaking faucets	
Paint	
DRAMATIZE	
Brighter lights	

Garage

NEAT	
Store all non-essential items	
CLEAN	
Floors – sweep clean	
Lighting fixtures	
REPAIRED	
Cracks in wall, garage floor	
Leaking faucets	
DRAMATIZE	
Neat shelves	
Hooks for hanging tools	
Brighter lights	

Den, library and recreation room

A den or a library is a plus. It should appear as a well-organized, cozy, private refuge where the buyers could envision themselves working. You do not need to take the same care with the recreation room as with the kitchen or family room; however, it is important to convey the overall impression that this is a well-kept home. At the very minimum, the recreation room should look neat with most things put away.

Den or library

NEAT	
Remove magazines, newspapers, books, etc.	
Arrange furniture to create an open feeling	
Remove extra plants, furniture	
CLEAN	
Carpet, spot or full clean	
Hardwood floors – shine	
Drapes, curtains, blinds	
Lighting fixtures	
REPAIRED	
Cracks in wall, ceiling	
Paint, wallpaper	
DRAMATIZE	
Large flower display	
Flower display	
NEUTRALIZE	
Light paint color	
Neutral wallpaper	

Recreation room

NEAT	
Remove magazines, newspapers	
Remove and store all non-essential items	
Arrange furniture to create an open feeling	
Remove extra plants, furniture, fixtures	
CLEAN	
Carpet, spot or full clean	
Hardwood floors – shine	
Drapes, curtains, blinds	
Lighting fixtures	
REPAIRED	
Cracks in wall, ceiling	
Paint, wallpaper	
DRAMATIZE	
Brighter lights	
Large flower display	
NEUTRALIZE	
Light paint color	
Neutral wallpaper	

Laundry room and backyard

A neat, clean laundry room reinforces the positive first image, that yours is a well-kept home.

Laundry room

NEAT	
Remove clothes, shoes, boots, etc.	
CLEAN	
Floors, sinks, appliances	
Curtains, blinds	
Lighting fixtures	
REPAIRED	
Cracks in wall, ceiling	
Paint	
Leaking faucets	
DRAMATIZE	
Brighter lights	
NEUTRALIZE	
Warm, light paint color	

Backyard and garden

NEAT	
Remove and store all non-essentials	
Toys, games, play areas	
Lawn cut and trimmed	
Bushes trimmed	
Flowers appropriately located	
No signs of pet activity	
CLEAN	
Patio area	
Walk and steps	
REPAIRED	
Patio area	
Walk and steps	
DRAMATIZE	
Large plant near steps	
Hanging flowers	
NEUTRALIZE	
Any negative features	
Any distracting ornaments	

SHOWING YOUR HOME

Think of all the packaging activity as preparing for the next step – the big event – the presentation of your home to buyers. This presentation may take place several times at open houses and private showings.

The first step is to show the home to the sales representative from your agent's office and to other sales representatives that he or she works with. The objective is to make as many sales representatives as possible aware of the home and get their feedback on the price and on how well the home shows.

The next step is an open house is for possible buyers (and inquisitive neighbors). Your agent will invite as many potential buyers as possible and other sales representatives will do the same. This open house gives your home maximum exposure.

In addition to these open houses, you should be prepared to show the home on weekends and sometimes with only an hour's notice through the week. People who have come in from out-of-town to look at houses may not have much leeway for rescheduling.

FINAL CHECK

Sight Everything is neat, bright and dramatized.

Smell No overpowering odors in the home unless it is the smell of cookies just baked and sitting on the counter. If necessary, spray a deodorizer through the home.

Sound Have the television off and a radio playing soft music, ideally, throughout the whole home.

The perfect buyer for your home is out there, right now, looking for it. All your work ahead of time will just make that buyer's decision a little easier.

For fifty years, Coles Notes have been helping students get through high school and university. New Coles Notes will help get you through the rest of life.

Look for these NEW COLES NOTES!

GETTING ALONG IN ...

- French
- Spanish
- Italian
- German
- Russian

HOW-TO ...

- Write Effective Business Letters
- Write a Great Résumé
- Do A Great Job Interview
- Start Your Own Small Business
- Buy and Sell Your Home
- Plan Your Estate

YOUR GUIDE TO ...

- Basic Investing
- Mutual Funds
- Investing in Stocks
- Speed Reading
- Public Speaking
- Wine
- Effective Business Presentations

MOMS AND DADS' GUIDE TO ...

- Basketball for Kids
- Baseball for Kids
- Soccer for Kids
- Hockey for Kids
- Gymnastics for Kids
- Martial Arts for Kids
- Helping Your Child in Math
- Raising A Reader
- Your Child: The First Year
- Your Child: The Terrific Twos
- Your Child: Age Three and Four

HOW TO GET AN A IN ...

- Sequences & Series
- Trigonometry & Circle Geometry
- Senior Algebra with Logs & Exponents
- Permutations, Combinations & Probability
- Statistics & Data Analysis
- Calculus
- Senior Physics
- Senior English Essays
- School Projects & Presentations

Coles Notes and New Coles Notes are available at the following stores: Chapters • Coles • Smithbooks • Worlds Biggest Bookstore

NOTES & UPDATES

NOTES & UPDATES

NOTES & UPDATES

NOTES & UPDATES